The BBC:

70 years of broadcasting

by John Cain

Published by the British Broadcasting Corporation
Broadcasting House, London W1A 1AA
Produced by BBC Information Services
Printed by Colourset Litho Ltd, Croydon, Surrey
© BBC 1992

Contents

'Those who cannot

remember the past

are condemned to

repeat it.'

George Santayana

The Life of Reason

Acknowledgements

In preparing this book, I have been much indebted to Lord Briggs, whose scholarly works, included in the reading list, constitute a comprehensive portrait of the BBC and with whom I have had the privilege of working in the preparation of the forthcoming Volume V of *The History of Broadcasting in the United Kingdom*. This outline draws heavily on his works. I owe a great deal to many other people, including Pat Spencer of the now disbanded History of Broadcasting Unit whose knowledge of BBC history is prodigious, the staff of the BBC Written Archives, Research Libraries and News Information Unit and Registries; Norma Gilbert and Suzi Higman for their picture research, Nigel Wright for his design, Leonard Miall, whose 1981 chart I have adapted and updated, Monica Atkinson and Monica Long for typing at great speed, Sally Hine who compiled the index and Richard Gilbert, the editor of the book. All of them saved me from errors and made useful and helpful suggestions for improvement. Obviously, I accept responsibility for any remaining errors in what follows.

John Cain

Introduction

The BBC, regarded by millions of people as the best and most influential broadcasting organisation in the world, celebrates its 70th birthday this year. 1992 is also the 60th anniversary of Broadcasting House and of the BBC World Service. This is therefore an appropriate time to look back at what has been achieved by the BBC, especially as the broadcasting landscape in the United Kingdom is changing so rapidly.

This outline history is intended to give the general public, and those beginning a study of the media in Britain, some understanding of the birth and development of what has been called 'the cornerstone of British broadcasting'. Any views are mine, as is the choice of topics.

It is a sketch and not a detailed portrait. For those who want more information, a reading list is provided. However, I hope that the date list and attached chart usefully supplement the text. The former includes the transmission dates of many important programmes, while the latter focuses on political, constitutional and administrative matters.

This book concentrates on programmes, people, policies and politics, and pays less attention to administrative changes and regional structures, important as these are to a full history. Inevitably, my choice of programmes mentioned, which could have filled the whole book, is subjective and some readers may miss certain favourites. The same applies to people, where I have chosen, for reasons of space, to pay what may seem undue attention to the roles of the Chairmen of Boards of Governors and the Directors-General. Broadcasting is a co-operative venture, and includes the support services as well as the producers and the senior executives.

Some readers may be surprised at the space given to engineering policies and practice, but I hope they will agree, in the light of the evidence, that this is an appropriate decision. Politics are inseparable from any discussion of broadcasting. The decisions of politicians of any party which holds power influence broadcasting output and structures more than many people care to admit.

1

forerunners

National broadcasting systems, involving both radio and television, are created and grow in ways which reflect local conditions – social, political and cultural. The BBC, a manifestly 20th-century institution, is one example among many different systems, all of which have their technical origins in the 19th century.

Post Office engineers check Marconi's equipment, after he established communication across the Bristol Channel in 1897.

Wireless broadcasting, or radio, started as a national service in Britain in 1922, 14 years before television. Both had a long technical ancestry. The work of scientists, inventors and engineers in many European and American countries came together at the end of the 19th century to make it possible for Morse code messages to be sent across space, using electricity and magnetism but without connecting wires. Originally, this wireless telegraphy was extremely crude and less efficient than sending messages along wires.

The principles employed by pioneers of wireless development, such as the Italian Guglielmo Marconi and the Englishman Sir Oliver Lodge

Guglielmo Marconi (1874-1937)

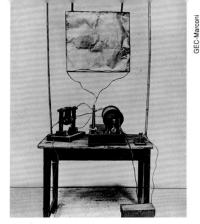

August 1895: Marconi achieves transmission over a distance of 1.75 miles using an earth and an elevated aerial at both the transmitter and the receiver

in the 1890s, had been worked out and published in 1873 by a Scottish physicist, James Clerk Maxwell, in the form of mathematical equations. Successful experiments showing that these mathematical 'ghosts' had an electrical wave-like reality were carried out in 1887 by a German, Heinrich Hertz. Behind this and much other work lay earlier fundamental discoveries. The principles of television were also understood well before anyone saw pictures at a distance. Marconi, who realised the commercial possibilities of sending messages over long distances by 'Hertzian Waves', came to England in 1896, managed to interest the British Post Office in his experiments

An experimental transmitter at Chelmsford – one of the places where British broadcasting had its beginnings.

with wireless telegraphy and secured important patents. The Marconi Wireless Telegraph Company was founded in 1900 and pioneered the setting up of transmitters and receivers throughout the world. At first, he and other enthusiasts were able to send only Morse code messages, since the technology was not sophisticated enough to handle music and the human voice. That would, eventually, require microphones, headphones and loudspeakers, among other things, but the invention of the telephone and gramophone were 19th-century forerunners.

In the first 20 years of the 20th century, much fundamental experimental work was done in nearly all the larger and more advanced countries. The aim was to develop the technology required for what we now think of as broadcasting – that is, sending a wide range of sounds, including the human voice and

GEC-Marconi

1914: Set used by Marconi between vessels at anchor 10km apart off Italy

It is both my belief and earnest hope that these Marconiphones, the latest popular development of the principles of my invention, may benefit the public at large by providing every home in the land with a new medium for education and entertainment

G Marconi

A personal message from Marconi in 1922 to wireless enthusiasts of the day

A remarkable Art Deco set, exemplifying Marconi's gift for anticipating trends and using his inventive genius

music, from powerful transmitters to thousands of individual receivers. As early as 1904, the British Government had passed the Wireless Telegraphy Act, recognising the need to control this potentially powerful new medium of 'mass communication' as it came to be called. Before this potential could be realised, components of the technology such as valves had to be invented and improved.

This was done largely in England, America and Canada. By 1914 the Marconi Co. had begun the transmission of speech, and wireless telephony became a practical reality.

Much of the know-how for true broadcasting was in place when the First World War broke out and, as often happens, war proved to be a powerful impetus to technical progress so long as it had military uses. For example, air-to-ground telephony became possible and the navigational use of wireless had also been appreciated. In the years immediately after the war, and with some of the inevitable military security restrictions relaxed, a huge popular interest developed in amateur 'radio', an American word which slowly supplanted 'wireless' in Britain, although the BBC in 1923 called its programme magazine *Radio Times*.

Developments generally proceeded at a much faster rate in the USA, which emerged from the war in a much healthier economic state than Britain. It was a large, sprawling, rich country, imbued with an entrepreneurial frontier spirit, and these factors encouraged piecemeal regional development, rather than a unified national one. The Post Office, acting as the agent of the British Government and as an 'honest

'Listening in' on a cat's whisker and crystal set during the Twenties

June 1920: Dame Nellie Melba in Britain's first advertised public broadcast gives a song recital from Marconi's works, Chelmsford

6: A. A. Campbell
Inton, a well-
wn electrical
gineer of the day,
oduces the
ing Marconi
William Preece,
gineering Department
ef, General Post Office

British Broadcasting Company Limited
Share Certificate No 11 issued in 1923

A mobile wireless set in use during the First
World War

broker', moved cautiously. It had learned lessons from the 'chaos of the ether' caused by the interference between signals from many different stations observed in the advertising-led system across the Atlantic. The advertisements were regarded as vulgar and intrusive, although advertising as such was not objected to either by the Government or by the future BBC.

A few large firms in Britain were given licences to broadcast experimentally in the early Twenties, and Marconi's stations at Writtle near Chelmsford and in London (with the code name 2LO) transmitted historic programmes between 1920 and 1922. Along with other stations in Manchester (2ZY) and Birmingham (5IT), London's 2LO later became an early BBC centre.

The 2MT transmitter at Writtle

The vital step in the formation of a national broadcasting system came in 1922, but at this stage no clear idea of what became public service broadcasting existed. The Government in that year licensed the six major radio manufacturers with other smaller companies to form a limited company called the British Broadcasting Company. This monopoly was financed by a Post Office licence fee of 10 shillings, payable by anyone owning a receiver, supplemented by royalties on the sale of BBC receiving sets made by the manufacturers. Since the BBC received only half the licence fee revenue, the other half going to the Treasury, and since few sets were sold at first, the new company's income was small. Nevertheless, British broadcasting was born, and quickly thrived. The first broadcast transmission was from London on 14 November 1922, but it remained to be seen what the working principles and practice of the new organisation would be. To begin with, the Government kept strict control over all aspects of the operation, particularly regarding broadcasts on 'controversial' matters. They were prohibited.

2LO masts on the roof of Selfridges,
Oxford Street, London

company years

Early difficulties, Reithian solutions

Clearly, the tiny new Company with its staff of four required a convincing policy. In the difficult postwar economic and political circumstances of 1922, that meant a strong leader was needed quickly. He was found in the shape of a 33-year-old Scottish engineer, John Reith, who was appointed General Manager on 14 December 1922 and started work on 30 December. From that moment John Reith was the architect of public service broadcasting in Britain. This was to become a system which stood between the unregulated American commercial one and the highly regulated system favoured by the then new Soviet Union.

Sir John Reith, the first BBC Director-Gene

John Reith dominated the BBC from the day of his appointment until his unhappy resignation on 30 June 1938. The Company had been formed officially on 18 October 1922 in an unstable social climate. Lloyd George's Coalition Government was about to collapse, the country was in serious debt and unemployment stood at 1.5 million. Few people, including Reith, had any experience of broadcasting and most members of the public were unaware of the potential of what was to become, in a few years, an important mass communication medium rivalling the press.

Many regarded 'listening-in', as it soon came to be called, as a craze which would quickly pass even if press, theatre and cinema-owners viewed the new

Arthur Burrows, first Director of Programmes

competitor with deep suspicion. How could they ensure the competition would be 'fair'? Evidently the situation demanded people with immense will, enthusiasm and energy if the new enterprise was to succeed. Reith had all these qualities in abundance but, with his strict Scottish Presbyterian upbringing, he could also be arrogant and autocratic.

In the long term, the challenge was to ensure the survival of the Company, which involved Reith in tough political and economic battles. The chief day-to-day problem facing him and his small staff, which included Arthur Burrows (the first Director of Programmes) and Peter Eckersley (the first Chief Engineer), both with rare experience at the Marconi Company, was to put together programme schedules to attract a growing audience. There was little to go on, apart from what the Americans had learned in a very different situation: no audience research (which came in 1936), no adverts to fill time or provide income and no competitor to provide a spur. Moreover, important constraints, apart from money, set limits to what could be done. News had to be supplied by existing agencies and,

1922: John Reith's application to become General Manager of the British Broadcasting Company

at first, bulletins broadcast only after 7pm to pacify the press. Political controversy was not allowed while writers, performers and musicians, sometimes backed by professional organisations, had to be wooed and trained in the ways of the new medium.

Captain Peter Eckersley, first Chief Engineer

The British Broadcasting Company's Certificate of Incorporation

The Savoy Hill Studio 9 and...

...Studio 1, elaborately decorated and draped

The 10-Shilling Receiving Licence
in 1923

Educate, Inform, Entertain

To make their programmes and broadcast them over the air, the small band of pioneers had to find studios, build transmitters and set up an administration, which soon operated from Savoy Hill in London's West End. They had strictly limited funds with which to do all this.

Reith's main objective was to provide the best programmes for rich and poor alike, and to eschew the shoddy, the sensational, the morally dubious. In this he was begging many questions which stirred up great controversy and still reverberate today.

Reith came to the view that these should be the three broad strands of British broadcasting but they had, in fact, been pinpointed earlier as the aims of public service broadcasting by American pioneers such as David Sarnoff. In the USA, however, an unregulated commercial system had, in Reith's eyes, destroyed this ideal and the result was triviality. 'Educate', 'inform' and 'entertain' are three words which have remained at the centre of the British system.

The first BBC daily transmission from Marconi House was, in fact, informative — a news broadcast about the General Election the following day. It was given twice, once slowly and once at normal speed, on 14 November 1922 by Arthur

'Listening in' in the early years

Burrows who, like many senior staff in those days, doubled up as broadcaster. It was not a news broadcast we would recognise today since the BBC had no news staff and the material came from established news agencies. Infusing many of the early programmes was a sense of seriousness, particularly on Sundays when they were generally worthy and dull. Religion and moral values were crucially important to Reith and he did his best to see that they were reflected in the schedules.

Within a year of his appointment the staff had grown from four to 177 and five stations across Britain had been added to those in London, Manchester and Birmingham. The first plays, concerts, charity appeals, debates, variety shows, weather forecasts, SOS messages, women's talks, dance band broadcasts, symphony concerts and religious talks had all been heard during that year by those people who had access to receivers. The Greenwich Time Signal, Big Ben and national broadcasts to schools soon followed in early 1924. Particularly significant at the time was the broadcast by King George V on 23 April 1924, speaking at the British Empire Exhibition, Wembley.

The good listener does not oscillate

Reith never regarded radio as something which should be 'on tap': he wanted listeners to be selective. In today's terms they had little choice, since programme schedules were typically restricted to about six hours in the afternoons and evenings with an hour-long concert in the morning. Especially important was the birth on 28 September 1923 of *Radio Times*, which quickly became an important source of information about programmes and a powerful public relations instrument. 'Listening in' was soon a popular pastime, a topic for conversation and a butt of the newspaper cartoonists.

Late Twenties: Marconi-Reisz microphone

September 28, 1923: First issue of Radio Times

Cellist Beatrice Harrison accompanying a nightingale with her cello. First broadcast 1924.

April 1927:The microphone in position for the first broadcast of the Oxford and Cambridge boat race

Round electro-dynamic microphone used at 2LO

Recording sound effects inside the studio

Philip Ridgeway's Young Ladies broadcast from Savoy Hill

The General Strike

Along with this popularity came controversy, as very soon the BBC came into conflict with political parties, religious groups, business interests and others. Inevitably, it was to prove impossible in a democratic, pluralistic society, to please all the people all the time. The politicians, in particular, would prove difficult and in 1926 Reith and the new Company were put to their first real test. The General Strike — the only one in British history — began on 3 May, and without regular daily newspapers, the BBC became almost the sole purveyor of news through five bulletins spread throughout each day, rather than being restricted to one evening bulletin.

For Reith the General Strike was both a baptism of fire and a challenge, given the restrictions on 'controversial' broadcasts. Would he be able to maintain even a measure of independence in reporting events between a Government determined to break the strike and a trade-union movement determined to win it? Opinions differ about the answer, but while many felt that Reith was too compliant towards the authorities, it is certainly the case that, at the very least, he succeeded in ensuring that the BBC survived to fight another day. He and his colleagues were put under enormous pressure, not chiefly by the Prime Minister Stanley Baldwin, who got on with Reith, but by others including Winston Churchill, the Chancellor of the Exchequer, who did not, and who wished the BBC to be taken over. His *British Gazette*, produced from 11 Downing Street, was the only real source of information apart from the BBC and it was, in effect, a Government propaganda sheet. There would have been nothing unconstitutional in a takeover by the Government, which had legal authority, under the Wireless Broadcasting Licence (1923) issued to the Company, to require the BBC to broadcast what it chose and also ultimately to control it. Technically, this remains the situation today, but for reasons of political diplomacy the Government's legal powers have rarely been used.

Crown Copyright

May 12 1926 : Front cover of *The British Gazette*

Crown Copyright

Before licences were issued the General Post Office authorised the use of wireless apparatus by letter.

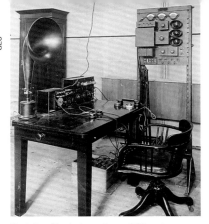

Control position instrument room GEC works,
Witton, Birmingham

GEC

Greenwich Time Signal and Tuning Note Apparatus

Blind listeners at St Dunstan's, Sussex

Off Centre

It would be a mistake to view the early BBC as a centralised, London-dominated institution. Daily broadcasts began from the Marconi Company's station 2LO in London on 14 November 1922, but transmissions followed from Manchester and Birmingham the next day. Newcastle opened up on 24 December and stations in Cardiff, Glasgow, Aberdeen, Bournemouth and Belfast joined in during 1923/4 to complete the network allowed under the Government's first licence. The non-metropolitan stations, with their own local advisory committees, were intensely independent, rather like the local radio stations which sprang up in the late 1960s. It was a matter of pride that local musical, dramatic and writing talent should be encouraged, but several of the early provincial station directors later moved to London to develop features, drama and other important broadcasting strands. Manchester and Birmingham were the first stations to broadcast children's plays.

Unfortunately there were at least two obstacles, one technical and one financial. The range of the early transmitters was often limited to 20-30 miles, so that many people were unable to receive broadcasts, especially if they owned the early crystal sets, which were popular but technically unsophisticated.

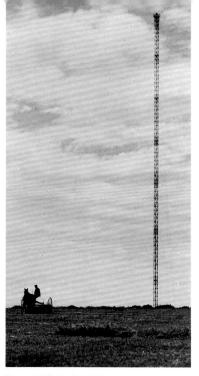

Daventry 5XX, the first high-power,
long-wave station designed for broadcasting

The 2LO control room at Savoy Hill

The first broadcast to schools with Sir Walford Davies in 1924

The solution was to set up 'simultaneous broadcasts' (marked SB in *Radio Times*) so that by using Post Office land lines and a number of newly-built low-power transmitters, one broadcast could be distributed widely through a network. This was an elegant solution to a technical problem, and also reduced programme costs. But not everyone was happy: it meant that less local talent would be used and London would be seen to be dominant. News occupied the first SB on 29 August 1923, and proved the power of wireless by bringing the nation together as a 'family'.

During 1923 and 1924, several more relay stations were opened in smaller British cities such as Sheffield, Leeds, Plymouth and Edinburgh. These stations were highly innovative with, for example, outside broadcasts from coal mines and factories. By September 1925, 40 million people could pick up BBC signals.

The greatest technical triumph of the Company during the period was the building of the first long-wave high-power national transmitter at Daventry (which lasted until 1992). Opened on 27 July 1925, Station 5XX was the biggest in the world and could transmit its signals to virtually the whole nation on 1600 metres.

Commentating on the first broadcast Derby in 1927

Changing Gear

The BBC's first Government Licence to operate had been designed to last until 1925, but decisions still had to be made about the long-term running of British broadcasting. Questions about the form of any new organisation and the possibility of any new competition needed to be answered. The Government responded as it had done in 1923 by creating a Committee. Then it had been the Sykes Committee, named after the Chairman Major-General Sir Frederick Sykes, set up after the Company had started work and charged with answering fundamental questions about broadcasting in Britain. Should broadcasting be entrusted to one or more organisations? Should it be a Government department or a private company under licence? How should it be financed?

Crown Copyright

The redesigned Receiving Licence in 1927

Now, in 1926, it was the Crawford Committee, chaired by Lord Crawford. These were to be the first of eight major Government Committees, which up to the present (and disregarding smaller enquiries), have examined the structure and running of British broadcasting.

Crawford's task was a difficult one, but so was Reith's, and he had a clear idea of what he wanted. Giving evidence to the Committee, the only member of the Company's Board to do so, Reith made it clear that he wanted broadcasting run as a public service under 'unitary control' and dedicated to the highest standards. Above all, he wanted a future constitution to ensure that broadcasters were as free as possible from political interference and from commercial pressures. One of his assertions was that broadcasting had potential for doing good or doing harm, so it should not be used solely to entertain, especially if the entertainment was, in his eyes, frivolous. Writing of his beliefs in his book *Broadcast Over Britain* (1924) he made the famous remark, much discussed ever since: 'He who prides himself on giving what he thinks the public wants is often creating a fictitious demand for lower standards which he will then satisfy'.

Leading artistes of the day, Lady Tree, George Grossmith and Madame Delysia broadcast in 1926

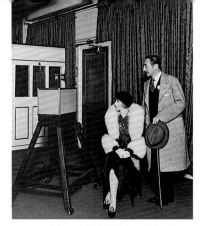

American film-star Adolphe Menjou and his wife at 2LO

'He who prides

himself on giving

what he thinks the

public wants is

often creating a

fictitious demand for

lower standards

which he will then

satisfy'

It seems that Reith was not opposed in principle to the idea of funding by advertisements, although he did not like the idea. He believed, correctly, that the newspapers opposed such a move since it would deprive them of income, and also give undue power to richer corporations able to afford advertising.

Given that the Government of the day was Conservative, the solution finally arrived at, following the recommendations of the Crawford Committee, appeared to some to be close to 'socialism'. The Company, a monopoly, was to be turned into a public service Corporation (not a Commission as Crawford suggested) and would derive its authority from a Royal Charter, complete with Great Seal, not from a statute passed by Parliament. Finance was to be by licence fee, still fixed at 10 shillings (but with an inadequate proportion, in Reith's view, going to the BBC) and with five Governors, appointed by the Government, providing the ultimate authority.

Reith was moderately happy with the general principles underpinning the new organisation but, apart from his disappointment at the financial arrangements, he was disturbed that the Government still opposed politically controversial broadcasts as well as the broadcasting of the proceedings of Parliament. Above all, he disapproved of the man chosen to be the first Chairman, Lord Clarendon (with whom he was to cross swords). This did not augur well for the immediate future.

The new Corporation was given an initial life of 10 years under its first Charter and it was officially born on 1 January 1927. Reith became Director-General and was given a knighthood, which he accepted after some deliberation and which appears to have given him little comfort. In later life he wrote:'I do not care two hoots or one hoot about honours, and often wish I had never taken one'. Nevertheless he took many.

3

Growth in Lean Times

The Company was dissolved in 1926 and its shareholders paid off. It had achieved much in four years, and the number of licences had risen to 2¼ million (the forecast was 500,000). The 10-shilling licence fee was generally regarded as good value, although it was a substantial outlay for some since the average weekly wage during that time was a few pounds. With the new arrangements in place and despite several disagreements between Reith and some of the new Governors, growth and development was even more spectacular in the late Twenties and early Thirties. Despite the economic depression of 1930 and 1931, licences were being bought at the rate of over 1,000 a day; by November 1932 4½ million were held. The figure had risen to 8½ million by 1938, by which time 98% of the population could listen in.

The early crystal and cat's whisker sets had been followed by valve sets, originally referred to in their more powerful form as superhets and heterodynes. By the early Thirties, the clumsy 'wet' batteries which powered these classical-looking creations were being replaced by mains power sets. These new streamline receivers cased in a new plastic, bakelite, sometimes designed by modern architects and industrial designers, expressed the most advanced ideas of the day and their appearance had much in common with the new Broadcasting House, which was to be opened in 1932.

Many people could not afford even the cheaper sets costing the equivalent of most of a week's wages, and, as early as 1924, there had grown up companies providing good reception by cable through a relay system. Others rented their sets or bought them by instalments. The age of consumer electronics had

Receiving Licence, 1929

1930s EKCO Radio

The End of Savoy Hill : A 1932 programme

The Two Leslies, a well-known musica
of the day

1932: Sir John Reith hands over the
keys of Savoy Hill to the
commissionaire

begun but, as always, the best and often the largest receivers (and radiograms) were marks of social superiority − status symbols. This became even more obvious when the BBC's television service began in 1936. Meanwhile, for numerous low-income families in the Thirties, the purchase of a wireless receiver was an economic and personal landmark.

The social effects of radio began to be obvious by the mid-Thirties. Working men and women were putting in 10 hours at the factory or office, and listening in as a family pastime grew, especially at weekends. People gathered together to hear national and sporting events. A new shape to the week was being created, assisted by *Radio Times*, which by 1939 had a circulation of three million. It became, and remains, Britain's best-selling weekly periodical. At a more intellectual level, and initially as a support to its educational programmes for adults, *The Listener* was first published in 1929, much to the dismay of other weekly rivals such as the *New Statesman* and *The Spectator*. It attracted a wide range of writers and critics right up to January 1991 when it ceased publication, falling victim to increasingly tough competition. Along with *Radio Times*, *The Listener* remains an invaluable resource in libraries as a mirror of its time.

1929: First issue of *The Listener*

Christopher Stone at the turntable in 1931

1930: Announcer Stuart Hibberd reading the news

The longest letter ever received by the BBC in 1938

Programmes and People

In the 1930s a pattern of listening was created which tried to satisfy all tastes from the 'highbrow' to the 'lowbrow', but which many in the population clearly felt put the emphasis on the 'high'. Letters to the editor of *Radio Times* complained of too many lectures (as talks were often called) and too much 'serious' or 'mournful' music, not the stuff for the working man after a hard day's work. Yet, given the temper of the time and Reith's fundamental beliefs in the need to lift people's sights, much was on offer. Many ideas, too, came from listeners and, within certain limits, Reith, his senior colleagues and the producers were always keen to encourage an exchange of ideas between the public and the Corporation. A Programme Correspondence Section was set up in 1924 to deal with the thousands of letters being received centrally every year, quite apart from those going to producers and *Radio Times*.

One suggestion taken up came from a listener in Watford: it was for a daily religious service, which began in 1928 and quickly became a fixture in the schedules at 10.15am. As radio listening became more popular and the number of licence-holders rose to three million, the idea of a reliable and fixed set of daily offerings, with some surprises, gained popularity. Many of these daily and weekly landmarks had been created in

A Radio Circles membership certificate

pre-Corporation days. Another predictable event of the day was *Children's Hour*, (in fact a 45-minute programme). Early versions had started in the Regions in late 1922 with imaginary 'Uncles' and 'Aunties' as presenters and these quickly became popular nationally. Many firsts can be claimed by *Children's Hour* which, through popular wireless clubs called Radio Circles, pioneered the idea of raising money for children's good causes. The first play specially written for radio was broadcast for children, as were the first stories told over the air. A different fixed period of time was also devoted to the inter-

A history lesson from School broadcasting, 1931

ests of children but this was for education rather than for entertainment. School broadcasts had begun nationally in April 1924 with a music lesson from Sir Walford Davies but, again, a regional station, Glasgow, had carried out experiments earlier. By the Thirties, School Broadcasting was well established and in 1938 it reached over 8,000 schools. Education was high on Reith's list of priorities and it is of considerable interest to note that the leading article on the front page of *Radio Times* of 13 June 1924 is enti-

The BBC's gardening expert, Mr C.H.Middleton

tled 'A Broadcasting University', while an article in the September 1927 issue was entitled 'The University of the Air'. In fact, it took until the Seventies for the Open University to be established, with broadcasts as an essential component of the teaching method. Back in the Twenties and Thirties, there were numerous serious lectures given by the famous, such as G.B.Shaw and H.G.Wells, and by the not so famous. One at least, John Hilton, became well-liked as a philosopher friend to the underdog.

A studio zoo broadcast

.C. Lyle commentates on the 1935
Grand National from Aintree

1935: Colonel Brand commentates at Wimbledon

American film star Gary Cooper and his wife
In Town Tonight

Perhaps the most remarkable speaker was Mr Middleton, who began broadcasting in *The Week in the Garden* in 1936 and continued talking in gardening programmes throughout the war, becoming a popular national figure.

As confidence in the BBC's ability to handle political and other controversial issues impartially grew, and despite charges of bias from the fringes of left and right, the Government's attitude towards control over broadcasting gradually changed. But the ban on 'controversial' broadcasts was not removed until 1928 and then only experimentally. It was now up to the Governors and the Director-General to decide what should be broadcast. *The Week in Parliament* began in November 1929, becoming a few months later the still-running *Week in Westminster*.

At a more popular and immediately more relevant level were the regular news bulletins, based at first on information provided by the news agencies but from 1932 put in the hands of an increasingly independent BBC news department. The proportion of time devoted to news doubled between 1927 and 1929 and together with the weather forecasts, the time signals from Greenwich and from Big Ben, they punctuated the listening day. Less frequently came the SOS messages, the market prices for farmers and *The Week's Good Cause*.

This last group of short transmissions, which all originated before 1927, were frequently referred to as service programmes and were clearly central to the public service philosophy. They have remained so. But entertainment was what the greater mass of the public wanted and they received it in increasing if insufficient quantities even during the Reithian regime. Music, drama, features, outside broadcasts such as sport, variety and talks all developed significantly from 1927 to 1938. Before this period the sporting authorities had refused to permit broadcasts for fear of attendance figures being seriously harmed.

The Savoy Orpheans broadcast from
The Savoy Hotel, London

Jack Payne and the BBC Dance Orchestra, in 1928

George Melachrino and his saxophone

Music had been the earliest and most popular staple fare of broadcasting, particularly dance music, although the chief pride of many in BBC management was the enlargement of serious musical taste in Britain before and during the war. Reith generally approved of dance music, unlike jazz, and it was first heard in 1922 (light classical music having been in the schedule from the beginning) although it was at first consigned to the later evening. The Savoy Hotel Orpheans and Havana Bands were popular outside broadcasts from October 1923, but later Henry Hall, with his BBC Dance Orchestra (which he took over from Jack Payne), became a major national figure. He returned during the war with *Henry Hall's Guest Night*, which had begun in 1934. His opening greeting, 'Hello everyone, this is Henry Hall speaking', was an early radio catchphrase and his signature tune, 'Here's to the Next Time', became a hit melody.

The BBC's efforts in spreading knowledge of and interest in classical music (including serious contemporary music) has been almost universally praised. The story is a complex one, but a few landmarks stood out even before the Thirties. In June 1923, the first symphony concert had been broadcast, followed in August 1927 by the first BBC Promenade Concert. The Proms had been inaugurated by Sir Henry Wood in 1895 and the BBC had come to their financial rescue. This proved to be probably the most significant single development in British music in this century and the Proms went from strength to strength.

The BBC Symphony Orchestra at Queen's

Dr Adrian Boult conducts the BBC Symphony Orchestra in 1936, the year before he was k

1934: Dr Adrian Boult (left), and Sir Edward Elgar's daughter examine the manuscript of the symphony commissioned by the BBC on which her father was engaged before his death

August 1927: Programme for the first BBC Promenade Concert

August 1927: Poster for the first BBC Promenade Concert

Novelist Agatha Christie visits the studio during the production of *Yellow Iris* to meet actor Anthony Holles (Hercule Poirot) and producer Douglas Moodie

Just as important was the setting up of the BBC Symphony Orchestra, which first broadcast under the baton of Dr Adrian Boult in October 1930. Boult, who was also the BBC's Director of Music and was knighted in 1937, made an immense contribution to the musical life of the country.

The BBC swiftly became Britain's major patron of music, including the commissioning of new music. Elgar's Third Symphony was dedicated to the BBC, making it, in the words of the *Daily Telegraph*, 'the first corporation ever to be inscribed in the title page of a symphony'. Other orchestras were formed in later years; opera was commissioned and performed; several series of talks on musical theory were introduced – all contributing to a huge programme of musical education.

Drama and features attracted a smaller but growing audience. In drama, where technical innovations using sophisticated electronics and other effects opened up new possibilities, the choice ranged from Shakespeare to the dramatisation of popular novels in serial form — a drama programme technique which gained in popularity and which is employed today in both radio and television. Radio, increasingly, was able with music and effects to create 'pictures in the mind', which later led to the observation that, as a medium, it is superior to television because 'the pictures are better'.

Radio was admirably suited to blending together dramatic and documentary elements. This led to the creation of a Features Department, which in 1936 grew out of the Drama Department that was led by Val Gielgud, the brother of Sir John Gielgud. Over the next 20 years the output in this field became prodigious under the guidance of a remarkable man, Laurence Gilliam.

Among the many outstanding programmes of the Thirties, tackling widely different themes, were *March of the*

Howard Marshall, a notable outside broadcast commentator, is remembered for his despatches from Normandy on D-Day

Freddie Grisewood became a BBC announcer in 1929, and chaired *Any Questions?* for 20 years

Microphone made for King George V's first broadcast message to the Empire, Christmas Day, 1932

King Edward VIII broadcasts to the Empire in 1936

45 (history), *Gale Warning* (descriptive 'actuality') and *Lepanto* (a literary work by G.K. Chesterton). Gilliam himself was famous for his Christmas features which incorporated the King's Speech in a fascinating mix of material. Some of the Features department output seemed dated, élitist and even patronising to some, but there is no doubt that a new radio 'art form', now taken for granted, had been invented.

Another new adventurous radio genre was the outside broadcast, which became highly popular. In particular the major sporting events won millions of armchair fans, listening to the commentators, another new radio word. Reith had wanted to broadcast what came to be called 'running commentaries' from the earliest days, but various interested organisations had delayed their introduction. It was not until the Thirties that the likes of John Snagge, Freddie Grisewood, and Howard Marshall became household names, reporting on Test cricket, the Boat Race, football and state occasions. A sad but unique broadcast was the Abdication speech by Edward VIII in 1936.

Variety, as it was then called, attracted the largest audiences. In many ways it was a 20th-century version of 19th-century music hall, and, indeed, one popular series of the period was called just that. Eric Maschwitz, the founding father of BBC Variety and a successful writer who created his own musical shows such as *Balalaika*, produced many of the programmes from a new BBC theatre in St George's Hall, opened in 1933 but bombed during the war.

Among the earliest variety programmes were *Songs from the Shows* and *The Kentucky Minstrels*, but the legendary successes of the late Thirties which created many of the first radio stars, performers and writers included *Monday Night at Eight* (a miscellany produced by Harry S. Pepper), *Band Waggon* (a situation comedy with Arthur Askey and Richard Murdoch) and *It's That Man Again* (with Tommy Handley). ITMA was

1938: The popular comedy series *Band Waggon* with Richard 'Stinker' Murdoch (left) and 'Big-hearted' Arthur Askey

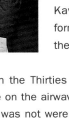

Crash! In the Broadcasting House effects studio during the Thirties

essentially English humour but was based on the faster-moving American style of comedy. It was written by Ted Kavanagh, who with Francis Worsley as producer, was to form with Handley a trio which brought enormous pleasure to the British public just before and during the war.

Gracie Fields at the microphone

But in the Thirties there were restrictions on the type of jokes that could be made on the airwaves. Written guidelines on what was acceptable material and what was not were issued to artists and producers. Jokes about drunkenness, religion, infidelity, effeminacy and human infirmities were unacceptable, as were racist references. On one occasion, in January 1935, a BBC news bulletin apologised for a lapse of taste in a variety programme: 'The BBC apologises to listeners for the inclusion in *Music Hall* of certain highly objectionable remarks, violating standards which have been firmly established by the practice of the BBC.' The remarks in question were exchanged between two comedians, Clapham and Dwyer, who said on air: 'What is the difference between a champagne cork and a baby?' 'A champagne cork has the maker's name on its bottom'.

Rehearsing a radio version of Shakespeare's A Midsummer Night's Dream

Anodyne material today, but in the mid-Thirties sufficiently controversial to get the comedy duo banned for five months. In 1939, the BBC's Head of Variety John Watt remarked: 'It is said that there are only six jokes in the world, and I assure you that we can only broadcast three of them'.

So popular were some BBC Variety shows that they were transferred to the theatre. Comedians revered by millions, just like TV stars of today, were Vic Oliver, Gillie Potter and Jeanne de Casalis, while Anne Ziegler and Webster Booth made up the first popular singing duo.

A live OB from London's Paddington Station

The new medium was no longer entirely dependent on the greater world of showbusiness; it could now generate its own writing, formats and performers which would later continue to feed into the approaching world of television.

Novelist H.G. Wells at the microphone in 1929

American film star Edward G. Robinson was among many famous names who broadcast in the thirties

The Broadcasting House news room in 1936

Well-known entertainers Elsie and Doris Waters (sisters of Jack Warner) take part in the 1937 *Coronation Party*

The Birmingham Control Room, 1931

Television Arrives

The BBC Television Service began on 2 November 1936. 'A mighty maze of mystic magic rays is all about us in the blue,' sang Adele Dixon in the opening programme.

Experimental television, Baird Studio. *The Man With The Flower In His Mouth* by Pirandello – the first play to be televised, in 1930

The idea of transmitting pictures over the air was almost as old as the telephone, invented in the 1870s. The essentials of the television transmission process, the sending of electrical signals down wires or across space, have much in common with those in radio. However, television carries an extra requirement, the breaking down of a visual image into small elements which can be handled electrically. Some 19th-century experimenters proposed ways to do this, but it was the rotating scanning disc, perforated with holes arranged spirally, patented in 1844 by a German, Paul Nipkow, together with the earlier discovery that the electrical conductivity of the element selenium was sensitive to light, which made television a practical possibility.

It was not until 1925 that a Scottish engineer, John Logie Baird, demonstrated the potential of a low-definition scanning system and, through energy and pig-headedness, fathered television in Britain. Baird achieved this with the somewhat reluctant help of the BBC, with whom he had an uneasy relationship.

John Logie Baird with a Nipkow rotating scanning disc, part of his television apparatus

Meanwhile, due largely to the invention of the cathode ray tube at the end of the 19th century, scientists in many countries were approaching the problem of scanning from quite a different angle. Little practical work on these lines was done in Britain though in the period 1908-11 an engineer, A.A.Campbell-Swinton, proposed and elaborated theoretically a system which proved to be a remarkably accurate prediction of how television would develop, replacing mechanical scanning by electronic scanning using a cathode ray tube.

Douglas Birkinshaw, later Superintendent Engineer, Television, with the Marconi EMI instantaneous television camera, at Alexandra Palace, London

Josephine Baker, televised with makeshift props and egg-shaped microphone in Studio BB, Broadcasting House

From the mid-Twenties onwards, Baird badgered the BBC to take television seriously, but there was considerable scepticism. Reith, who had attended the same technical college in Glasgow as Baird, regarded television as a device which deflected attention and energy away from radio development – and he also disliked his fellow-Scot.

But the BBC held a broadcasting monopoly and by 1929 it was obliged to allow experimental transmissions. These achieved wide publicity in the press but the 30-line low-definition picture was small and indistinct, and very few people owned a receiver. Baird, who was tenacious, continued to improve his apparatus, and in August 1932 the BBC, in more positive mood, inaugurated its experimental service, using a studio in Broadcasting House. The programme items on offer in 1933 included a review, some animals and boxing, but few members of the public had access to these pictures.

Emitron camera tube, 1936

Unfortunately for Baird, his competitors, using electronic scanning, were making rapid progress. The EMI company, which had links with research in America, developed an 'Emitron' camera tube based on earlier work by the Russian Vladimir Zworykin, who had emigrated to the USA. This offered a clearer, high-definition television picture. Events now moved quickly and a Government committee, chaired by Lord Selsdon, issued a report in January 1935 recommending that the BBC should operate a television service for the public. An interesting proposal within the report suggested that both systems should be tried out in alternate weeks as a trial. On 2 November 1936, Baird, using a much

Part of the original 1936 Alexandra Palace TV transmitter

improved version of his system, found himself in competition with EMI, which had joined forces with the Marconi Company. The world's first regular high-definition television service had started, although the Germans had begun their low-definition service in March 1935, using a mechanical scan system. Hitler was probably the first politician to recognise the potential of television for propaganda purposes.

It soon became clear that Baird's system was inferior, and in February 1937 it was dropped, leaving the field to the EMI-Marconi electronic system which, with many improvements, is used to this day.

'The Bomb' condenser-type microphone, introduced in 1934

Between 1936 and 1939 a wide variety of programmes was offered. News, plays, ballet, opera, magazine programmes, outside broadcasts, cartoons and concerts all flickered across the 10-inch screens of the 20,000 households in the London area which possessed television receivers. *Picture Page*, the most popular programme of the period, was an early example of the now familiar magazine format. It introduced many public personalities to the screen, and TV stars began to emerge. Joan Miller, Jasmine Bligh, John Snagge and Leslie Mitchell were among them. Technicians, producers and presenters all learned to work in the medium between 1936 and 1939 and their experience proved

smine Bligh, at the phone unit, Studio oadcasting House, London

Jasmine Bligh, one of the main pre-war television announcers

Eric Wild and his Teatimers with Claire Luce, in the floor show *Pastiche*

1937: The camera follows the progress of King George VI's Coronation Coach during BBC Television's first major outside broadcast

American Sophie Tucker, one of many famous music-hall stars who brought their talents to the television studio

invaluable for the future. The public, in increasing numbers, bought licences which remained at 10 shillings until 1946.

The Television Service was suspended in 1939 for defence reasons and the technical staff were drafted to work on radio. The transmitter at Alexandra Palace from where the Service operated would also have provided German bombers with a good direction-finder to London.

The last prewar programme, a Mickey Mouse cartoon, was transmitted at noon on shut-down day, 1 September 1939. Nobody could predict when or if the television service would open again. Only the wealthy could afford television receivers at a price of about 100 guineas and there were many sceptics in the BBC hierarchy at Broadcasting House.

It was not until 7 June 1946 that BBC Television returned and from then onwards the story took a different turn.

Listener Choice

Reith and his senior colleagues had always wanted to give the BBC audience a wider choice and, clearly, the best ways of achieving this were to vary the programme output as much as possible and to open up new channels. The first of these depended on producer imagination and good scheduling, the second on the engineers. Since it was politically and socially important to encourage non-metropolitan talents, the concept of regional broadcasting seemed to be the answer. Several powerful transmitters would be needed, each covering a large area of Britain. A regional programme schedule would replace the original, restricted, local programme schedules. With the National programme transmitted from Daventry, all listeners would then have a genuine choice.

Work on the Regional Scheme, as it came to be called,

began in 1926 under Peter Eckersley, the BBC's Chief Engineer, but completion did not come until well into the Thirties. The technical problems were exceedingly complex, especially as the increasing crowding of the air waves was inevitably coming under international control. For example, in 1926 the Geneva Plan had formulated agreements on wavelength allocation between countries.

Slowly but surely, impressive, large, gleaming new transmitter stations opened up in London (at Brookmans Park to replace 2LO), in the North (at Moorside Edge) and in the West and Midlands as well as in Scotland and Ireland. One of the most famous was that at Droitwich, opened in 1934, which replaced Daventry as the transmitter of the National Programme. At the time, these technical marvels were described as temples of science, and with them went new Broadcasting Houses, the headquarter buildings in each region. The most famous Broadcasting House was that in Portland Place, London, which became the BBC's central headquarters in May 1932. A Latin inscription, still in the

front entrance, refers to 'This Temple of the Arts and Muses...' and at the time Broadcasting House was indeed an artistic achievement architecturally, a prime example of art deco. However, not everyone agreed and, as often happened in BBC matters, controversy raged. One critic called the building 'a petrified dreadnought' while another guardedly referred to it as 'a product of our epoch'. All who used it agreed from the start that it was too small.

The first Regional Head was appointed to the North Region in Manchester in September 1928. All the Heads of Regions were responsible for their own programming. Tensions inevitably grew up between them and the central London management, but, increasingly, the regions became renowned for their programmes, both in terms of quality and innovation. Many, such as the famous *Scrapbooks*, produced originally by North Region, later became national favourites, while several series from outside London addressed social problems such as unemployment in ways which did not always please the establishment.

The Droitwich transmitting station in 1934

George Bernard Shaw meets the cast and er of his play *How He Lied to Her Husband* during ak in television rehearsals. On the left: the young unknown Greer Garson

The original television control room, 16 Portland Place, London

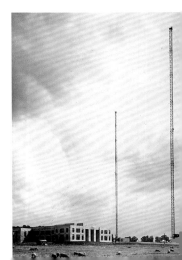

Broadcasting House

Broadcasting House became the headquarters of the BBC on 1 May 1932, although the first broadcast from there, Henry Hall and the BBC Dance Orchestra, had taken place on 12 March. The new prestigious building replaced Savoy Hill, off the Strand, which had been the BBC's home since 1923, and contained three times as many studios, although with the rapid expansion then occurring in broadcasting, it quickly became too small. Sites had been considered in the Haymarket, Park Lane and Trafalgar Square, but the one at Foley House at the corner of Portland Place and Langham Street, due to be developed as a block of flats, was eventually chosen.

The shape of the site and the need for the most up-to-date studios determined the design of the building which became an example of art deco, then a fashionable style. The architect, G.Val Myer, worked with the BBC's civil engineer, Marmaduke Tudsbery, who was responsible, among many things, for the sophisticated air-conditioning system which controlled both the temperature and humidity. The positioning of the studios in a central core maximised the sound insulation.

There were many unusual features inside and outside the building, notably the sculptures by the distinguished artist Eric Gill, and the studio interiors by several modern designers such as Wells Coates and Serge Chermayeff. Since the Thirties there have been many changes to Broadcasting House, but the marbled entrance hall, the Concert Hall and the Council Chamber – all designed by Val Myer – have retained most of their original features. The studios have been redesigned and re-equipped and, in the process, the Thirties decor, after reflecting the use to which the studios were to be put, has gone.

The original Broadcasting House, which now has an extension built between 1957-61, is a grade II listed building.

erving the Empire

During the Twenties, the British Empire was still the largest in the world. For centuries, British men and women had gone to remote places taking with them their political, cultural and religious ideas, usually ruling but, increasingly, delegating power and authority. Reith, a patriotic man who had fought in the trenches in the First World War, felt from early in his BBC career that broadcasting could help to keep the links strong between those at home and those who had gone to Africa, Canada, India, Australia and other parts of the far-flung Empire.

Although experimental broadcasts by the BBC in 1927 had been welcomed, it was not until December 1932 that financial and technical difficulties were overcome and an Empire Service started.

Apart from the desire to make links, it was already clear that such broadcasts would encourage the building up of broadcasting systems in the dominions and colonies themselves. Later they would counter the often propaganda-laden messages coming from other countries such as Italy and Germany.

As often happens in broadcasting, the obstacles in the way of a fully-fledged service were technical, financial and political. Before signals could be sent over the huge distances involved, short-wave transmitters and receivers would be needed. These would cost money, and few governments like spending money on untested projects, especially when they have political implications overseas.

Front page of the Empire Broadcasting bulletin, 1937

Although eventually persuaded by the case for an Empire Service, the Government was not at first prepared to pay, especially in the harsh economic climate of the early Thirties. Since the sums involved were modest, the BBC decided to go ahead under its own steam, using a new short-wave transmitter at Daventry. The programmes, too, cost relatively little since they were largely repeats of programmes made for the home listener. This, incidentally, gave

MONDAY (September 20)

choslovakia)
4 m.) ; 32 kW.
vals from 6.30 a.m.
nan Transmission.
.20—Art Review.
35—For Workers.
Prague. 7.15—Jazz

ava.
ague.

No. 1)
(Belgium)
9 m.) ; 15 kW.
—Records ; Gym.

—Salon Orchestra.

sic by the Radio
nductor: Doulies.
Russian Music. 2.0
55—News. 5.0—
6.0—Talk : The

hery (Violin) and
(Songs), Violin :
son). Songs: (a)
Melodies (Stekkee,
Pierne). (c) Floods
smaninov), Violin :
lanse (Dupuis), (b)
eis (Kreisler), (c)
(Falla).
Siegfried Idyll
kish March, "The
me " (Beethoven).
Review ; Aviation
News.
The Clock Sym-

Commemoration
al Orchestra. Con-
de Thoran, with
er). Emma Luart
sprenne. Part I.
ould. Part II.
25—Talk : Pierné.
.10–11.0—Brenders

No. 2)
(Belgium)
m.) ; 15 kW.
ernish.
—Records ; Gym.
—Records. 12.31
nestra. 1.0—News.
nestra. 1.10—

BUDAPEST (No. 2)
(Hungary)
359.5 kc/s (834.5 m.) ; 18 kW.
7.0 p.m.—German Lesson. 7.30—
Talk. 8.0—News. 8.25—Records.

COLOGNE (Germany)
658 kc/s (455.9 m.) ; 100 kW.
Transmits at intervals from 5.50 a.m.
12.0 noon—Concert. 1.0 p.m.—
News.
1.20—Concert from Hamburg. 2.0
—News ; Riddles. 3.0—For Children. 3.45—Markets.
4.0—See Leipzig. 4.30—Talk 4.45
—Songs of Many Lands—Soprano.
5.15—Art Talk. 5.30—Waltz Records.
6.30–7.45—See Munich. 7.45—Talk
8.0—News. 8.10—Weekly Review.
9.0—Johanne Unkel (Contralto).
Josefa Kasterul (Violin), Rummel
(Pfte.). Fantasia and Fugue in
G minor (Spes). Two Songs
(Heuser). Suite (Lemacher), Im-
provisations (Riethmüller), Three
Songs (Heuken). Romance and
Ländler (Siegl). 10.0—News.
10.30–12.0 m't—Light and Dance
Music—Station Orchestra, Glahe
Band.

DEUTSCHLANDSENDER
(Germany)
191 kc/s (1,571 m.) ; 60 kW.
Transmits at intervals from 6.0 a.m.
12.0 noon—See Leipzig. 1.45 p.m.
—News.
2.0—Variety. 3.0—Exchange ; Programme Notes. 3.45—Books.
4.0—Light Orchestral ; at 5.0 —
Reading. 6.0—Records.
6.30—See Munich.
7.0—Berlin Philharmonic. Conductor : von Kempen. Willi Stech
(Pfte.). Military Symphony
(Haydn). Spanish Rhapsody
(Ravel). Excerpts, " The Damna-
tion of Faust " (Berlioz). Over-
ture, " Käthchen von Heilbronn"
(Pfitzner). Indian Fantasia (Bu-
soni). Don Juan (Richard Strauss);
at 8.0–10.0—News.
9.0—Topical. 9.15—Records. 10.0—
News.
10.30–12.0 m't —Light Orchestral.
Conductor : Aulich.

Sketches. 3.10—AVRO Orchestra
Conductor : Treep.
4.10—Talk by Max Tak, with Re-
cords : French Music. 5.10—Kovac
Lajos Orchestra. 6.10—AVRO
Dance Band. 6.40—Records. 7.20
Greta Breyne-Dicken (Songs. 7.40
—News. 7.50—Records. 8.40—
" The Inspector Investigates "—
Detective Programme.
8.50—AVRO Orchestra, Conductor
Treep. Borovsky (Pfte.). Con-
certo grosso (Handel). Pfte. Con-
certo in B flat (Beethoven.
9.40—Reports. 10.0—Palla (Organ
Markman (Songs). 10.40—News
10.50—AVRO Dance Band. 11.20
11.40—Records.

HILVERSUM (301.5 m.)
(Holland)
995 kc/s ; 15 kW until 5.40 p.m.
60 kW from 5.40 p.m.
NCRV Programme.
7.40 a.m.—Bible Reading ; Medita-
tion ; Sacred Music on Record.
8.10—Records ; at 9.10—Greeting.
10.10—Religious Programme. 10.4
—Religious Address. 11.10—Re-
cords ; at 11.40—Announcement.
12.40 p.m.—Gray (Organ). 1.40—
For Schools. 2.10—Report. 3.10—
Records. 3.25—Bible Reading. 4.2
—Records ; For Children. 5.25—
Mlle Welters (Pfte.). 6 ''' , ' '''
Announcements . 5.40—Talk
Review. 7.50 (approx.
(Organ). 8.55—Talk :
dam Salon Orchestra.
Kiekens at 9.40—P
and at 10.25—Gym.
Records ; Bible Reads

KALUNDBORG
240 kc/s (1,250 m
Relays Copenhagen
(255.1 m.).
Transmits at intervals t
12.0 noon–2.0 p.m.
chestra. 2.30—Dresm.
2.40—Reading (Pär La
—Petersen Orchestra.
less Notes. 5.0—Talk
and John Dewey. 5
5.40—Exchange ; Mar
8.50—Canzona : Dou

An issue of *World Radio*

A translator/announcer dictates a news
bulletin for the Arabic Service

impetus to a technical development which was to revolutionise broadcasting — the recording of programmes. The alternative was frequent live repeats. 'Bottled' programmes, as they were initially called, became increasingly common in the Thirties, which explains the increasing number of archival recordings still available from that period.

The first transmission took place on 19 December 1932, aimed at Australia; on Christmas Day, King George V gave the first broadcast to the Empire by any monarch. After the success of this event, the Empire Service was given an allocation of £100 per week for its programme costs. Soon there were broadcasts occupying several hours a day to five different areas of the Empire, and in 1935 the Government was sufficiently impressed to agree that official funding would be needed to help with the capital and recurring costs. Today, the World Service, successor to the Empire Service (which began in Broadcasting House), operates from Bush House in London, part of which the BBC has occupied since 1940. Funding comes not from the licence fee but from a grant-in-aid voted by Parliament. Editorial control rests with the BBC but the Government determines not only the languages in which the Service can operate but also the number of hours in which each broadcasts.

In this respect a key development occurred in the Empire Service when, with war looming, it was decided to offer a service in Arabic, the first broadcast being transmitted on 3 January 1938. The Italian Government under Mussolini was using a powerful transmitter to broadcast to the Middle East, and its propaganda had to be answered in the measured and balanced tones which have given the BBC's external broadcasting such a high reputation worldwide. As we shall see, more valuable work was accomplished in the war, proving Reith's original vision to have been vindicated.

King George V makes his first broadcast to the
Empire on Christmas Day, 1932

End of an Era

Marconiphone 12-inch mirror-lid receiver, 1937

When he resigned in 1938, Reith, physically unwell, was downcast. There were many reasons for this, particularly the worsening of his relationship with the Governors. Although his relationship with his Chairmen had improved since the days of Lord Clarendon, he felt he did not always get from the Board the support he deserved. While recognising that the Governors had responsibilities as 'trustees in the national interest', he always wanted these to be 'general and not particular' responsibilities. He craved a new and more powerful job, was frankly growing weary of the BBC, of some of his colleagues, and of the many committee meetings he had to attend. He felt that, having put the BBC on its feet, he deserved something better.

Reith's diary, which he kept diligently, has an entry for 16 November 1935: 'I do feel so tired of the BBC'. In 1938, having had resignation much in his mind for two years, he was offered the Chairmanship of Imperial Airways and he reluctantly accepted, probably seeing it as a stepping stone to something bigger. Even the manner of his going displeased him since the Board of Governors did not involve him in selecting his successor, an academic, Frederick Ogilvie. Typically, once gone, Reith felt he had made a mistake. He was not, as he always wanted, going to be 'fully stretched'.

Over the years, a number of difficult policy decisions had taxed even Reith's energy. These included a major administrative reorganisation of senior staff in 1933, criticism from both political parties in 1934 (which he answered successfully), and the preparations, begun in 1938, to put the BBC on a war footing, ready for the worst eventuality.

Two other issues which perplexed him, and which brought him into conflict with some colleagues, were listener research and staff relations. The resolution of both had long-term implications for the BBC.

Thirties example of moving coil loudspeaker

BBC Listener Research at work

Microphone and wooden hand grip
for OB use, 1930s

By instinct, Reith was paternalistic, and although he encouraged listeners to express their views to the BBC, he feared that reliance on measuring the size and composition of audiences by research would tend to inhibit the imagination and craftsmanship of production staff. Moreover, the interest of minority groups could easily be ignored in favour of the interest of the majority who, he believed, might be more unthinking, less reflective. Those of Reith's colleagues who argued for research were aware that the BBC was not, in the mid-Thirties, providing enough lighter programming to satisfy the mass public. Reith preferred to think in terms of publics, some of them small groups within the mass public.

But, in increasing numbers, listeners were turning to Radio Normandie and Radio Luxembourg, commercial stations which provided a constant stream of lighter entertainment in the racy American style, and which had to measure their audiences for the good commercial reason of selling advertising space. They were able to claim up to 80% of the audience on a dull BBC evening. After more debate, Reith lost the argument and a Listener Research Section was formed in October 1936. This was to prove a significant move.

In 1935, when the Corporation's first licence was within two years of expiring, another Government Committee of Enquiry under Viscount Ullswater was set up to consider the future. It reported in February 1936 and in general gave the BBC a clean bill of health, although it criticised dull Sunday programming, again strengthening the case for more light entertainment. One of the members of the Committee, Clement Attlee, a Labour MP and future Prime Minister, also drew attention in a minority report to what he considered an inborn bias in the BBC's reporting, citing the coverage of the General Strike. More importantly for the long term, he chided the BBC for its unfair staff relations and urged the encouragement of trade-union membership.

The Blattnerphone apparatus used by the BBC in the early Thirties. It recorded on steel tape

Reith felt that he treated his staff well and probably most of them agreed with him, but there was a small, vocal groundswell for less 'paternal' goodwill and more 'brotherly' goodwill. Discussions took place on setting up staff associations rather than fully fledged trade unions, but progress was delayed by the onset of war. In the meantime, personnel procedures for matters such as recruitment and training were improved. The BBC was experiencing the inevitable pain caused in any organisation by expansion and it was to suffer much more of this during the war. By then, however, it did not have Reith's undoubted energy, administrative skill and integrity at its disposal.

Recording the King's speech on a wax disc at the opening of the World Economic Conference in London, June 1933

war effort

1939-1945

Preparations for a War of Words

With the death of Marconi in 1937 and the end of Reith's leadership of the BBC in 1938, the two major figures of British broadcasting had passed on in their different ways and it was to prove difficult in Reith's case to find a replacement. The BBC required a war leader but, unlike the nation, it did not get one. After a short, indecisive period, Churchill replaced Chamberlain in May 1940, but in the mild-mannered Frederick Ogilvie the Corporation found itself in 1938 with a new Director-General who was unable to provide the leadership needed and after four years in office he was required to resign. The Board of Governors was reduced to a rump of two at the beginning of the war after the Government had been persuaded not to dismiss them all. Luckily, the Chairman, Sir Allan Powell, provided continuity until the end of the war, by which time the Board had returned to its prewar strength of seven.

These unsettling events were set against and partly caused by difficulties with the Government's censorship restrictions, the need to disperse out of London to safer regional centres, and a huge turnover in staff,

Frederick Ogilvie, Director-General of the BBC, 1938-1942

mainly due to call-ups. For example, the BBC Symphony Orchestra was moved to Bristol at the outbreak of war, and School broadcasting moved to Evesham in Worcestershire. Above all, a dramatic increase in the hours of broadcasting

ttings refer to the start of the French, German
and Italian Services

provided for the home audience, the Forces and listeners abroad meant that staff numbers increased from about 5,000 in 1939 to 11,000 in 1946, but this had the advantage of bringing in bright new people. The consequent administrative strain was immense, as the Second World War was to become a war of words, the first in history in which broadcasting was the main instrument of propaganda. Winning this aspect of the war effort meant that the BBC, like the nation after Dunkirk, experienced its finest hour and it established a reputation for telling the truth, as far as that is possible in wartime.

The overseas audience now became as important as the home audience. Programmes in Arabic had begun in January 1938, aimed at a target audience of 40 million. Then as now, oil in the Middle East, and the Suez Canal, were of vital strategic importance. The second phase in the development of the BBC's foreign language service began in March 1938 with broadcasts to Latin America in Spanish and Portuguese, followed six months later, as the Munich crisis developed, by the start of the European service, giving news in French, German

Televising the arrival of the Prime Minister, Neville Chamberlain, at Heston airport, on his return from his historic meeting with Adolf Hitler in 1938

and Italian. One year later, when Chamberlain made his speech on 3 September declaring war on Germany, Spanish and Portuguese broadcasts to Europe were added, along with an Afrikaans service and English lessons in the Arabic service. The main theatre of the European war, along with countries on our sea-trade routes, were now covered by broadcasts from Britain, and Bush House in the Aldwych became associated with them. In the following two years, most other European and Asian languages joined the growing list.

By 1945 the number of foreign language services grew to 40. It is not difficult to understand why the staff numbers increased, but easier to forget that many of the newcomers were foreign nationals. In wartime conditions, the security clearance problems were considerable.

T.S.Eliot (seated) and George Orwell (behind) take part in a wartime BBC Eastern Service programme

Listening in to what foreign broadcasters were saying, especially if they were enemies

The Forces Programme helped morale

BBC monitors listen in to wartime European broadcasts

or potential enemies, was as important as broadcasting to foreign countries. The Government had begun doing this at the time of the Italian/Abyssinian War of 1935, but in 1939 it asked the BBC to take over the activity and so the BBC Monitoring Service was born. Its purpose was to gather news and information as rapidly and economically as possible. Employing several hundred 'monitors', many of them refugees, the service quickly expanded so that it could 'listen' 24 hours a day to all the European languages likely to be of wartime use. The service was invaluable, too, in helping with the compiling of news bulletins and this remains true today, as events in Eastern Europe have shown.

While there was expansion abroad, at home the radio services were contracted to one, the Home Service. Earlier experience in the late Thirties and the planning which preceded the war had shown that such a service would be needed, first to keep the public informed and instructed about such things as evacuation plans, rationing, etc, and also to help maintain morale. The new Home Service replaced the National and Regional programme services, a move achieved by putting into operation a careful and ingenious engineering plan, whereby all the transmitters in the network operated on the same medium wavelength. This ensured that if one transmitter was damaged by German bombers, others could take over. It also frustrated the use of transmitters as navigational radio beacons by bombers.

By the time the Home Service opened, however, it had become clear that some special and separate programming was needed for the thousands of British troops assembling in France as the British Expeditionary Force. Not only was it likely that they would become bored and demoralised while they waited for action throughout the winter of 1939/40, but they would also become angry if they could not have something like the programmes coming from the commercial station Radio Normandie operating from Fécamp in northern France. At first the Government resisted the idea, but BBC managers argued strongly and with the help of senior army officers, relevant Government ministries were persuaded and relented. Experimental broadcasts to the troops started on 7 January 1940 and quickly developed into a 12-hours-a-day medium-wave

operation, the Forces Programme. It was to be a great success with both the Forces and the home audience, and contained important lessons for the postwar BBC.

Jack Warner (second left), in a group rehearsing for *Garrison Theatre*

Haw-Haw, Bombs and Other Hazards

In the early months of the war there was considerable criticism of BBC programmes on the new Home Service, mainly on the grounds that they were dull and uninspiring. At the same time German propaganda was achieving some success, however superficial. It appeared to many in what has been called the 'phoney-war' period before the real fighting and bombing in Western Europe began, and before Churchill took charge, that the enemy had stolen a march as far as propaganda was concerned. Goebbels, Hitler's 'Minister of Public Enlightenment and Propaganda', had been practising the black art of manipulating news for many years while appeasement was dominant in British politics and the BBC was concerned, not always successfully, with presenting a more balanced and truthful account of events.

Actress Valerie Hobson interviewed for *Monday Night at Eight*

Major Richard Longland talks to the troops about BBC Forces' programmes

William Joyce, 'Lord Haw-Haw', who broadcast German propaganda

Hulton Deutsch Collection

To listeners in Britain, the voice of Lord Haw-Haw became a familiar sound, evoking both apprehension and amusement at the same time. Although not the first man to whom the title was given, William Joyce became Haw-Haw and presented himself, illegally as it happens, as an Englishman who saw that

Author and broadcaster J.B.Priestley, whose *Postscripts*
to the evening news became legendary

Nazism was best
and predicted that
the decadent West
would fall to Hitler. He
was, in fact, a vicious
anti-Semite and former follower of Oswald Mosley's British
Union of Fascists, who remained true to his beliefs until the
end, when he was hanged as a traitor. But his broadcasts
from Radio Hamburg, which lasted from September 1939
to April 1945, proved damaging to morale in France and
Britain. It was always difficult to counter this sort of broadcasting with measured accounts of the truth, especially
when that truth was painful. One response was ingenious
and successful. The BBC, in February 1940, started broadcasting *Postscripts* to the nine o'clock news, which later
became legendary through the voice of J.B.Priestley.

It was clear that some kind of exceptional wartime control
would be needed, but the question was, what form would
this take? It had long been understood that a Ministry of
Information would be needed, and that its relationship with
the BBC would be a complex one, but such a Ministry came
into existence only 10 days after the outbreak of war when
the reduction of the BBC Board of Governors to two was
announced. There was some confusion for several months,
often resulting in arbitrary interference. The BBC Chairman
made it plain he accepted that the Government must have
the last word in matters relating to the war effort. A political
row followed in which Clement Attlee, soon to become Lord
Privy Seal in Chamberlain's War Cabinet and later Deputy
Prime Minister, vigorously questioned a policy which
seemed to emasculate the BBC. When Sir John Reith was
asked by Chamberlain to become Minister of Information in
succession to the first incumbent, Lord MacMillan, in
January 1940, he was not overjoyed. The Ministry was held
in low esteem by almost everybody and had become an
object of ridicule. Reith noted 'it was in notorious disre-
pute', and Tommy Handley, the BBC comedian, was able to
refer to it obliquely as 'The Ministry of Aggravation and
Mysteries'. When Churchill, no friend of Reith's, was made
Prime Minister, he brusquely asked Reith to become
Minister of Transport. Reith agreed without enthusiasm, not
having enjoyed a period during which, he observed, he had
been hailed as Dr Goebbels' opposite number.

1940: A delayed action bomb damaged Broadcasting House, killing seven people

Wartime newsreader and announcer, Bruce Belfrage

Gradually a tolerable way of working together was achieved between the BBC and the new Ministry of Information. Lines of responsibility for home and for overseas programmes were laid down, liaison officers or 'advisers' appointed, and the control of propaganda to enemy countries put, unknown to the BBC, in the hands of a secretly funded Government organisation known as EH (for Electra House where it was stationed). Later, in September 1941, Brendan Bracken, arguably the most able Minister of Information, and with a greater understanding of the BBC's difficulties than his predecessor, Duff Cooper, made many improvements. These included encouraging the removal of Ogilvie as Director-General and the setting up of a secret Political Warfare Executive (PWE) which replaced EH and was concerned more explicitly with propaganda to enemy countries, unlike the BBC. The PWE had its own transmitter.

The German blitz-bombing campaign against Britain, including London and other cities, began in August 1940 after the fall of France, and the BBC did not escape. BBC buildings, sandbagged and provided with sleeping accommodation in offices, were a prime target for the Luftwaffe and on 15 October 1940 a delayed action 500lb bomb fell on Broadcasting House in London. The well-known newsreader, Bruce Belfrage, paused in the nine o'clock news as he heard the bomb go off, but for security reasons did not react on air. Seven people were killed and the building badly damaged. Worse was to come on 8 December when a landmine exploded in Portland Place. Fire raged for seven hours and the BBC's civil engineer described the building as 'a scene from Dante's Inferno.' Earlier in September St George's Hall was damaged by fire, and was totally destroyed on 10 May 1941. The war was reaching the Home Front in earnest.

Wynford Vaughan-Thomas, one of the BBC's distinguished war correspondents

The Home Front

News was of paramount importance and the people, in blacked-out homes, rationed and tense under the bombing, listened avidly to the six daily bulletins. Announcers gave their names so that listeners would recognise their voices and be sure it was BBC news. The nine o'clock news became a particular focus of attention, with half the nation regularly tuned in to well-known voices such as Wilfred Pickles, the first newsreader with a regional accent. It was a sign of the

Frank Gillard files his historic despatch for *War R*◄ from the Normandy beachhead in June, 1944

times that Pickles, a Yorkshire character actor, should be used in this way and that the sound of a 'non-BBC' voice should have created controversy.

The first national newsreader with a regional accent: Wilfred Pickles

Those at home wanted to know what their friends and relatives in the Forces were doing, and in this way the sense of a 'people's war' was fostered. Later, radio was able to further this idea with request programmes. The flow of news was not normal, as individual branches of the armed services operating under very difficult conditions imposed their own private censorships, independently from the Ministry of Information. Some would have preferred complete silence. As the war developed, a team of distinguished war correspondents was built up, including Richard Dimbleby, Frank Gillard and Stanley Maxted, which brought to homes and factories exciting and often harrowing accounts of what was happening on the various fronts.

'Midget' disc recorder used throughout the Second World War

Petty Officer Jack Watson with guest artist Jessie Matthews in *Navy Mixture*

ITMA, with its star Tommy Handley (left), and members of the cast

...y, who became BBC Director-General in April 1944

Sandy Macpherson, the popular BBC organist

Several strands of entertainment programmes kept up morale. Many programmes created stars and several lasted for many years. At the lighter end, Tommy Handley's *It's That Man Again (ITMA)*, written by Ted Kavanagh, became the top comedy show. It began in July 1939 and ended in January 1949, its star dying a few days later. Unusually the Director-General of the time, William Haley, gave a microphone tribute to Tommy Handley, probably the most popular man in the country after Churchill. The programme had not been 'soft'. It was among the first to pillory civil servants and politicians (and, of course, Hitler and Mussolini) and one of its characters, 'Colonel Chinstrap', was a parallel to Low's newspaper cartoon character, Colonel Blimp. When a voice in the show said, 'Zis iss Fumf speakink', everyone knew that Lord Haw-Haw was being parodied. Moreover 'That Man' became synonymous with Hitler. Here was a new type of quick-fire comedy which amused the listener and laughed at the enemy (both within and without) simultaneously.

Other popular comedy shows on the Home Service were *Garrison Theatre*, which starred Jack Warner, and *Hi, Gang!* with Bebe Daniels, Ben Lyon and Vic Oliver while *Monday Night At Eight,* the Thirties miscellany programme, continued to draw big audiences. The Forces Programme, later in the war, brought early performances from David Jacobs and Jimmy Edwards in *Navy Mixture.* Many of these shows produced popular catch-phrases.

Forces' sweetheart Vera Lynn rehearses songs for *Sincerely Yours*

Variety output increased enormously during the war and included musical series such as *Sincerely Yours* with Vera Lynn, and those designed primarily with specific audiences in mind, like *Workers' Playtime* and *Music While You Work,* which sought to ease the grind and boredom of work in munitions and other factories. *Desert Island Discs,* still going strong, began in 1942.

Musical programmes of all kinds became one of the most effective ways of raising the spirits of the listeners, and there was plenty to choose from. *The Spectator* on 23 July 1943 noted: 'Whatever else it may have destroyed, the war has undoubtedly re-created music in our midst, affirming it a living force vital to the needs of the people.' After an unfortunate two-year gap, the Proms under Sir Henry Wood returned in 1941, now at the Albert Hall following the bombing of the Queen's Hall. Hundreds of music-lovers had to be turned away because of their popularity.

The BBC Symphony Orchestra under Sir Henry Wood plays at the 1942 Promenade season at the Royal Albert Hall

At the more practical and informative level were programmes which sought to provide facts and suggestions to help the public cope in wartime. *Can I Help You?* which started in 1939 — a precursor to *You and Yours* in the 1970s — was a kind of citizens' advice bureau of the air; countless cooking and food programmes helped to make life easier for families suffering rationing and other war restrictions, while the Radio Doctor, Charles Hill, began giving his invaluable medical advice in 1942. In the Sixties he was to become the BBC's Chairman. C.H. Middleton's *In Your Garden* and *The Kitchen Front* combined pleasure with advice on overcoming food shortages. At a

Workers' Playtime, broadcast from an aircraft factory with the well-known duo of the day, Scott and Whaley

more serious level were programmes which attempted to stretch minds and imaginations, like *As I See It,* a platform for those whose views differed from the Government's, and *Industrial Forum,* the equivalent for the factory floor of the military news contained in *War Commentary.* A surprising hit was *The Brains Trust,* an unscripted discussion which set people talking about a wide range of subjects and which lasted until 1949. The resident philosopher C.E.M.Joad was well-known for his opening words in response to many questions: 'It depends what you mean by...'.

The original team and question master of the weekly *Brains Trust,* celebrate their fifth anniversary on 1 January, 1946

The audience for radio drama doubled during the war, and *Saturday-Night Theatre,* started in 1943, was a regular date for millions. *The Man Born To Be King,* written for children by Dorothy L Sayers in 1941, became a radio classic, despite causing a storm by its depiction of Christ as an ordinary person. Other religious innovations were the short *Lift Up Your Hearts* (scheduled next to *Up in the Morning Early,* the physical jerks programme designed to ensure a healthy mind was contained in a healthy body), and *Before the Ending of the Day,* a devotional 15-minute programme which, every few weeks, closed the day's listening.

Man Born To Be King: A play sequence specially written for *Children's Hour,* by Dorothy L. Sayers

Professor John Hilton, who chaired *Industrial Forum*

From the early days of the war, the BBC provided education series for the armed services on a wide range of subjects, many linked to the war and the shape of the post-war world. These built on the group listening movement which had operated in the Twenties and Thirties. In 1945, a special Forces Educational Unit was set up under the wing of the Schools department to deal more specifically with the problems of postwar rehabilitation. The programmes ranged from history to the problems of Civvy Street.

Prime Minister, Winston Churchill, makes one of his famous wartime broadcasts

One surprising innovation was the rise of the inspirational straight talk. Many programmes of this genre were broadcast in the war, some quite individual and distinctive. The master was probably Churchill who first broadcast as Prime Minister on 19 May 1940, delivering his great rally to arms. Although no lover of broadcasting or the BBC, which he would like to have controlled, Churchill in his speeches had a simple vocabulary and straightforward but intense and considered delivery which gripped the patriotic hearts of ordinary people. In a totally different way the Yorkshire voice of the novelist and playwright J.B.Priestley began to attract mass attention from June 1940 onwards in the *Postscripts* he contributed to the Sunday-evening news bulletins. Priestley spoke of the aspirations of ordinary people. He was not afraid to criticise authority, a line which gave credence to the freedom of the British airwaves, and he had the audacity to express social and

Alistair Cooke began sending his *Letter from America* in 1946

political views very different from those of Churchill. The size of the postbag testified to his following, yet by October 1940 he was taken off the air, briefly to return in 1941, after protests by Conservative MPs who objected to his left-wing views.

In 1946, just after the war was over, another quite different but equally remarkable broadcaster, Alistair Cooke, began sending his *Letter from America.* That country was to play an increasingly important role in determining what happened in many aspects of British life in the succeeding years.

Resistance

It is difficult to imagine the sense of isolation and hopelessness experienced by those countries under German and Italian occupation. Millions of people turned to what a *Punch* cartoonist in August 1941 described as 'The Secret Hope': the radio. Others listened and acted against the enemy as part of the Resistance. These two groups existed in all European countries, including Germany and Italy, and later in other theatres of war. The radio, and this

War correspondent Stanley Maxted with the BBC recording car at München Gladbach, Germany, in 1945

normally meant BBC radio, was listened to clandestinely and on pain of severe punishment, instilling hope by providing vital information and advice. Since the object was to achieve victory, the messages often fell short of the objectivity aimed at in traditional BBC broadcasting and became propaganda. It took some time for the technique to be learned.

Punch

The Secret Hope

When the war started, many European foreign language broadcasting sections of the Empire Service were well established. A team of experienced Free French journalists and intellectuals was already operating when the comparatively unknown General de Gaulle broadcast to France for the first time on 18 June 1940. He was to make many such broadcasts, aimed at stiffening the resolve of those compatriots who had not fallen in with Marshal Pétain. The fact that Frenchmen were divided and that de Gaulle was regarded with suspicion by many indicates one of the difficulties experienced by broadcasters in dealing with resistance movements. Much later, this was to become a particularly difficult problem in the case of Yugoslavia, where the Communist and non-Communist factions of the resistance movement were fighting each other as well as the Germans.

The most imaginative and unplanned initiative of the war was to be the V broadcasts. These originated in the mind of the BBC's Belgian programme organiser, V being the first letter of the word victory in both French and Flemish, the official languages of Belgium. He introduced the V sign in a broadcast to Belgium, without anticipating the emotional response it would bring. Soon 'V for Victory' appeared everywhere in Europe, usually in chalk or paint, largely due to the efforts of Douglas Ritchie, an assistant news editor who assumed the name of 'Colonel Britton' when he began his V campaign broadcasts on 6 June 1941. Later Churchill exploited this symbol of victory in the familiar two-fingered gesture, the ambiguity of which gave added potency. In a broadcast to Europe on 19 July 1941, he remarked: 'The V sign is the symbol of the unconquerable will of the people of the occupied territories and a portent of the fate awaiting the Nazi tyranny.'

General de Gaulle broadcasts to his fellow countrymen and women in France on 30 October, 1941

War Correspondents Richard Dimbleby and Charles Gardner
edit a recorded news item

"Here is your request number, Sergeant Smart—'The Teddy Bears' Picnic'!"

Punch

Broadcasts from London had used the Morse Code V, three dots and a dash, as part of the campaign. But it was the Germans, worried by the possible effect of the broadcasts, now in several languages, who appropriated the V sign for themselves in station signals, and broadcast the opening bars of Beethoven's Fifth Symphony which matched the Morse signal.

Hugh Carleton Greene, German Editor during the war, became Director-General in 1960

Eventually official military fears that the V campaign was a mixed blessing, mainly because it seemed to encourage premature revolt from unarmed and badly armed civilians, brought it to an end in May 1942.

The setting up of the Political Warfare Executive by the Government led, in 1941 and 1942, to a much improved propaganda effort operating outside the BBC. For example, jamming of enemy broadcasts became more widespread, as did the use of 'black' propaganda transmitted from British sources while purporting to come from inside France and Germany. The BBC, properly, could never bring itself to distort the truth in the manner of Goebbels, but it did transmit messages to underground resistance fighters, especially as D-Day approached.

Crown Copyright

Coded messages to the French Resistance Movement, 1943

These messages were occasionally inserted in coded form into talks given by the Radio Padre, but also appeared in French service transmissions from 1941 onwards as *messages personnels*. Often sounding nonsensical, these privately agreed coded signals gave instructions regarding sabotage operations or parachute drops.

The Rev J.W.Welch and Radio Padre, the Rev Ronald Selby Wright, broadcasting from his script

In late 1942 and 1943, as the war reached its climax, broadcasts to Germany itself became even more important, despite heavy jamming, and took many forms apart from news, including drama and features. Dissident and disaffected Germans listened to the BBC in large numbers and in the autumn and winter of 1945 the audience reached an estimated 10 to 15 million a day. The man who led the BBC German service was Hugh Carleton Greene who, after the war, helped to reorganise German broadcasting and in 1960 became, arguably, the second most famous Director-General of the BBC.

Germany awake! Correspondents Stanley Maxted and Robert Barr find the writing on the wall in 1945

Turning Tide

As D-Day, 6 June 1944, approached, it became clear that the Allies were within sight of victory. Fresh tasks began to loom for the BBC, which now had a new Director-General, William Haley, a distinguished journalist who later became editor of *The Times*. In February 1944, a new General Forces Programme was set up to replace the previous Forces Programme which the general public, as well as the troops, had taken to. It was designed for a new situation – to enable servicemen and their families, through broadcasting, to experience D-Day and its victorious aftermath. The BBC introduced a special news service, and all the intricacies of intelligence and propaganda came under the control of the Supreme Headquarters Allied Expeditionary Force (SHAEF) which had its own broadcasting service and Psychological Warfare Department. There were links with the BBC and the American Forces Network, which had begun to transmit from within Britain in July 1943.

Richard Dimbleby (left), outside Hitler's underground bunker in Berlin

As the landings in Europe took place and the advance continued, a team of experienced BBC correspondents was formed into the War Report Unit. These men vividly reported 'actuality' from all the main fronts. *War Report* became an important broadcast after the nine o'clock news. Evocative commentaries covered the fall of each great city to the Allied armies, and the signing of the Armistice by the Germans was covered by Frank Gillard who had been with General Montgomery. Later, and in a quite different mood, Richard Dimbleby described what he felt as British troops entered the concentration camp at Belsen.

Broadcasts about Sir William Beveridge's Report on Social Security upset some MPs

1944: King George VI broadcasts his Christmas Day Message to listeners around the world

On VE-Day, 8 May 1945, Broadcasting House was bedecked with the flags of the 22 Allied nations and floodlit for the first time in eight years. Rejoicing was the mood that dominated the day's programming, which began with a fanfare and a personal message from Churchill. The Listener Research Department reported the highest rating for programme satisfaction ever recorded.

The flags of the victorious Allies fly at Broadcasting House, on VE Day, 8 May, 1945

The BBC had for some time been considering its peacetime future, hardly knowing what the difficulties ahead would be, especially those caused by the significant General Election of July 1945, which produced a Labour victory. There had already been many talks and discussions about the way British society might change after the war. Even broadcasts about the 1942 Report on Social Security, written by Sir William Beveridge, which was to become so important in debates about the welfare state, had upset some MPs. The omens for peace on the broadcasting front were not altogether good.

Bush House

Bush House, on an island in the Aldwych facing towards Kingsway, is the home of the World Service, and the only one of the three main BBC buildings in London not completely owned or occupied by the BBC. At the end of the last century, the area near Fleet Street and the Strand contained bad slums which were cleared by the old London County Council. In 1920 permission was given for the building of Australia House and Marconi House on the Aldwych island site, with the centre of the island reserved for the Bush Terminal Co. of New York. The owner, Irving T. Bush, planned luxury accommodation for manufacturers to show their wares to buyers worldwide, and the grand centre block, designed by an American, was opened in 1923. For economic reasons the four wings were modified for more conventional office use. Sculptures above the main Aldwych entrance, also by Americans, symbolise links between the English-speaking peoples.

The BBC first leased part of Bush House in September 1940 during a particularly difficult phase of the war before Broadcasting House had been badly damaged. New accommodation was urgently needed for the expanding European services and space in the south-east wing was adapted to make a studio. After bomb damage at Broadcasting House, the European service was evacuated to a temporary home in Maida Vale, but finally moved to Bush House in early 1941. In 1944 Bush House suffered damage from a flying bomb and one of the figures in the main sculpture over the entrance lost its left arm. After the war Bush House increasingly became the home of the External Services, as the Empire Service was then renamed.

Today the corridors, offices and studios of Bush House echo with myriad foreign languages, and the building, now owned by a Japanese organisation, is probably more familiar to more people worldwide than Broadcasting House and Television Centre.

5

recovery

1945-1955

Reorganisation For Peace

In the BBC Yearbook for 1945 an article entitled 'The Voice of Liberty' appeared. It was written by Georges Bidault, the French Minister for Foreign Affairs, who had been a prominent figure in the underground resistance movement, and it paid a moving tribute to the BBC's wartime broadcasts. The words *Ici Londres*, and the messages that followed, had acted like a compass to a sailor, guiding, assuring and saving from despair those fighting the enemy clandestinely. Broadcasting House and Bush House contain similar tributes in the form of tapestries, vases, plaques and sculpture, given in thanks by European broadcasters and others.

There was also renewed thankfulness in Britain in 1945, expressed through broadcasts on 15 August, VJ-Day, by King George VI and by the new Labour Prime Minister, Clement Attlee, who had come to power less than a month earlier. Nearly a year later, on 8 June, the great Victory Parade was televised by the revived Television Service, which had opened up the previous day with the same cartoon that had ended transmissions in 1939.

In a speech called 'Postwar Broadcasting' given in November 1944, Director-General William Haley had warned that 'Victory is now everywhere recognised as only a beginning. It is the great preliminary. It is what we manage to build following the exertions of these six long years that really matter. Of nothing is that more true than of broadcasting'. Haley had replaced Robert Foot, a businessman who, in turn, had shared the Director-Generalship with Sir Cecil Graves, ex-Deputy Director-General to Sir John Reith. These wartime arrangements had not been satisfactory for anyone, both Foot and Graves having resigned, and Haley now had a formidable reorganisation task ahead of him, involving domestic radio, Overseas and European radio (the word Empire was no longer appropriate) and the rebirth of television. All this was to be accomplished in a stricken economy, and with the first Labour Government in history enjoying a big majority in the House of Commons, intent on pushing through an extensive programme of social rehabilitation and reform.

The first signs were promising for the BBC. In the summer of 1946 the licence fee, which had been static for 24 years, was doubled to £1 and the BBC's Charter, the document which ensures its existence, renewed for five years. The latter was a mixed blessing because the expectation might have been that the extension would be for 10 years, as had happened in 1937 for the Second Royal Charter. There had, however, been enough support in Parliament for a large-scale enquiry into broadcasting to justify the reduction and an enquiry duly came in 1949. One of the chief issues now raised by people such as the ex-Director-General Frederick Ogilvie, as well as many MPs, was that of the BBC's monopoly. Was it to be 'foisted on us for a further term?' Ogilvie asked in a letter to *The Times*. The BBC celebrated its Silver Jubilee in 1947 with large questions hanging over it concerning its next Charter renewal, due in 1952, and its place in a possibly new broadcasting scene. The parallels with 1992, as the 70th anniversary was celebrated, are striking. The BBC is not new to danger.

Family listening in the Forties

Haley's chief personal interest was in radio, and its reorganisation became the BBC's top priority. Changes in the structure of the programme output were

June 1946: Postwar Victory Parade

effected rapidly. On 29 July 1945, Regional broadcasting, which had ceased in 1939, resumed and the Light Programme began, replacing the General Forces Programme. It inherited the characteristics of that network, as its title indicated, and was hugely popular, its share of the audience listening-time in 1945 reaching well over 50%. By 1948/9 the Light Programme was listened to on average for 9.5 hours a week. The Home Service, providing a richer middle-of-the-road output, could claim 7 hours

Mrs Dale's Diary with Douglas Burbidge and Ellis Powell

Gardeners' Question Time goes on air from Rochd

Dick Barton – Special Agent (played by Noël Johnson, left), in the popular thriller serial

The listening panel invited to comment on the first *Woman's Hour* included film star Deborah Kerr (left)

a week. Both networks were on air all day until midnight, the Light starting at 9am, 1½ hours after the Home.

Haley was not university-educated, but his interests were bookish and he believed high culture should be more accessible to more people. This belief lay behind the creation of the Third Programme in September 1946, the postwar innovation most closely associated with him, although discussions about a three-part structure for BBC Radio, with 'culture' occupying the third part, had taken place since 1942 when Haley joined the Corporation as editor-in-chief. There was no suggestion that each of the three networks was to be devoted to a single type of output but rather that each should compete in offering a 'mix' at a distinctive, targeted level. Plays, talks and music, together with programmes about public issues, would appear in each, and their audiences would constantly find themselves

'stretched' or at least surprised. Curiosity and understanding were central, and movement up the cultural scale was taken for granted as an ideal objective. Reith's influence still flourished in the late Forties.

The titles of some of the remarkable programmes of the period make the point. At the lighter, some would say lowbrow, level were many family favourites such as the action-packed thriller serial *Dick Barton, Special Agent*, the comic variety show *Much Binding in the Marsh* with Kenneth Horne and Richard Murdoch, set in an imaginary RAF station, *Housewives' Choice*, and *Mrs Dale's Diary*, one of the earliest family serials. This was to be joined in 1951 by *The Archers*, which like *Woman's Hour* still runs. *The Archers*, from the start partly intended as a service to farmers, was first made and transmitted in the Midland Region in 1950, but moved to the Light Programme in

The first series of Reith Lectures was broadcast by philosopher Bertrand Russell in 1948

School team representing Cardiff against Helsinki in *Top of the Form*

Round Britain Quiz quizmasters Gilbert Harding and Lionel Hale

1951, while *Woman's Hour* had been the name of one of the first British Broadcasting Company offerings. For the more inquisitive there was *Twenty Questions*, *Round Britain Quiz* and *Top of the Form* while *Listen With Mother* was a joy for those with a young family.

In contrast, the Third Programme offered a wide range of operas, plays by Shaw, Pirandello, Brecht and Sartre and talks by a wide range of contemporary thinkers. A new translation of *Faust* by Louis MacNeice (poet and BBC producer) was specially commissioned. Much of the Third Programme material was published in *The Listener*, which reached a peak circulation of over 151,000 in 1949. But there was some criticism, too, either from those who thought the output too highbrow or from those academics who were not invited to broadcast.

For the Home Service, in the middle ground, current affairs was the heartland with *The Week in Westminster* and *Today in Parliament* as regular slots. The nine o'clock news remained a vital national 'meeting point', and a notable innovation in 1948 was the first series of *The Reith Lectures*, which was to become an annual event in honour of the first Director-General. The first series was given by Bertrand Russell on 'Authority and the Individual'. At the more entertaining end of the spectrum were old favourites like *In Town Tonight* and *Children's Hour*. But there were also plays by Shakespeare, Ibsen and others, as well as *Saturday-Night Theatre*, which attracted audiences of over 12 million in the late 1940s. Two successes from this period, which still run, were *Down Your Way* and *Gardeners' Question Time* which began as *How Does Your Garden Grow?*

Robert MacDermot (left), who introduced the first *Housewives' Choice* in 1946 was again in the studio playing listeners' requests for the programme's 10th anniversary

16-inch disc player used to record radio programmes in the late Forties

For most people the mixture worked well most of the time, but there was less 'channel-hopping' than had been expected. The Third Programme was an obvious target of criticism for the less demanding public and mass circulation newspapers, while there were also complaints at the disappearance of wartime programmes with an American flavour. As often happens in such matters, there was a class bias in the listening pattern across channels and the Listener Research Department's work began to demonstrate this.

Take It From Here with Jimmy Edwards, Joy Nichols, Dick Bentley

Other worries and questions related to Regional broadcasting, despite the fact that many successes of the period came from the Midlands (eg *The Archers*), the West (eg *Any Questions?*) or the North (eg *Have a Go*). How much regional autonomy was London prepared to allow? How much strictly local programming was appropriate? Should the Regions be encouraged to contribute to the National network? Why was reception so bad in remote or mountainous areas? Above all, and predating the continuing debates about national identity, should Scotland, Wales and Northern Ireland have something approaching devolved broadcasting systems? All these and many other questions were addressed by the Committee on Broadcasting, set up by the Labour Government in 1949 and chaired by the distinguished liberal thinker Lord Beveridge, who had been made a baron in 1946.

Television Resurgent

'Our general

conclusions

are that

television

has come

to stay'

By 1955 the BBC was spending half as much on television as on sound broadcasting and the audience for the new medium was seriously eroding the radio as well as the cinema audience. The turning-point was probably the enormous success of the carefully planned television coverage of the Coronation in June 1953 when the ceremony was broadcast live and transmitted to Europe. The sale of black and white television sets, costing about £90, increased, and between 1951 and 1954 the number of combined sound and vision licences (at £2) had doubled to well over 3 million. The audience for the television coverage was said to be 20 million, far outnumbering the radio audience, but with most people viewing outside their own homes. If this surprised many observers, it also annoyed those enthusiasts in the Television Service who, in the immediate postwar period, were trying to recreate it on a budget of something like one-tenth of that given to sound broadcasting and could see the potential of the new medium.

2 June 1953: A clutch of international commentators (the BBC's Wynford Vaughan-Thomas on the right) describes the Coronation procession of Queen Elizabeth II

To be fair, official thinking had begun in the war when a committee had been set up under Lord Hankey to consider 'the reinstatement and development of the television service after the war'. Special consideration was to be given to research and development and to the manufacturing of sets 'with a view especially to the development of the export trade'. Both Baird and Isaac Shoenberg, who had led the Marconi-EMI team, as well as Gerald Cock, the BBC's first Director of Television, gave evidence and, when the report was published in 1945, the message was, on the whole, positive. Paragraph 78 proclaimed: 'Our general conclusions are that television has come to stay', and the BBC was recommended as the service provider, starting in London and six 'populous' districts.

Giselle, performed for television by the Ballet Rambert

The 1948 Olympic Games held in London was the first to be televised

1950: Richard Dimbleby in Calais commentates on the first television transmission from across the Channel

The experts assemble at Alexandra Palace for the 1950 General Election results programme

The 1948 logo of *BBC Television News*

Robert Dunnett interviews a visitor for the 1951 magazine programme *Festival Scotland* during the Festival of Britain

The aim was to achieve rapidly a technical standard comparable with that of cinema and much attention was focused on large-screen reproduction of television programmes. Entertainment, education, news and the televising of public events (that is, outside broadcasts) were all high-lighted. Eventually all these strands appeared, some more quickly than others.

The great successes were the public events, including sport and those focusing on Royal occasions. As had happened in the early days of radio, sporting organisations such as the Football League and the Boxing Board of Control were opposed to television and, indeed, did what they could to prevent the televising of events under their control. Ultimately money was to be the deciding factor.

News on television presented particular problems and began simply with a reading of sound news: news in vision did not begin until July 1954. This remarkable situation well illustrated the very cautious attitude that some BBC officials took towards the new medium. *Television Newsreel*, emanating from the film department and starting in January 1948, was the main 'news' component in the early schedules and although popular it was hardly 'news', being more in the style of cinema newsreels, with items usually distant from the headlines.

There were many originations, however, in the first five post-war television years, including the first television weather forecast, the first televising of the moon through a telescope, the first televised report of General Election

Picture Page, the first television weekly magazine programme, with presenter Joan Gilbert (left)

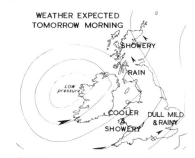

Television weather chart used when forecasts were first introduced in 1949

Television Dancing Club, with Victor Silvester and his Ballroom Orchestra

Children's television favourite *Muffin the Mule* shares a secret with Annette Mills

results and the first live television from France. 1951, the year of the Festival of Britain when the Government encouraged the people to give themselves 'a pat on the back', saw the first television party election broadcast, a programme genre which has not endeared itself to the public.

Among the really popular successes before the end of 1950 were *Mr Pastry* (played by the comic Richard Hearne), *Muffin the Mule* (the first TV character to become a favourite with children nationally), *Television Dancing Club* (with Victor Silvester) and *Come Dancing* (still running). For those seeking information, culture and activities, there was *Inventors Club*, Philip Harben's first cookery programmes, the *First Night of the Proms* and *Matters of Life and Death* about health matters. Among the new presenters were Fred Streeter and Percy Thrower, who followed in the footsteps of Mr Middleton, Joan Gilbert, an editor and presenter who had

worked on *Picture Page* before the war, McDonald Hobley, Elizabeth Cowell and Sylvia Peters. These personalities and others like them were to become synonymous with the BBC for most viewers.

In the first half of the immediate postwar decade the Television Service had made steady progress from its base at Alexandra Palace. By 1950 the hours of broadcasting had risen to over 30 a week and between 33% and 50% of the population was within reach of a transmission signal. There were, of course, wide geographical variations in ownership of sets and the ability to receive programmes, with outlying and mountainous regions being at a disadvantage, but by the time commercial television began, 50% had become 92%. Both in terms of engineering progress and programme success, the years between 1945 and 1955 were remarkable, despite close-downs in 1947 caused by a dramatic fuel crisis.

London Calling Overseas

During the war, the title 'Empire Service' grew more and more inappropriate as a description of broadcasts aimed at audiences outside Britain. Apart from the fact that the word 'Commonwealth' gradually became more acceptable to describe the loosely-knit group of countries making up the Empire, which were soon to achieve independence in increasingly large numbers, the scope of the broadcasts was now much wider. By the end of the war, there was a flourishing European Services Division and an Overseas Services Division that continued transmitting to a huge range of countries both inside and outside the old Empire. The Monitoring Service also remained very active within the Overseas Service Division, as did the Transcription Service, beginning as a small operation in 1932 to send 'bottled' or recorded programmes for rebroadcasting by radio stations in the Empire. By the end of the war it had grown through success and in 1953 was distributing 650 radio programmes and 100 telerecordings and films to countries round the world.

Despite a weakening of resolve by the Government in the mid-Forties over the question of financing overseas broadcasting, it became clear that the postwar task was to reinvigorate an idea discussed during the war. The aim of overseas broadcasting should be 'the projection of Britain'. This meant among other things broadcasting about British cultural life, its science and technology and its political institutions to all who wanted to listen. But the earlier ambition to serve the Empire, albeit in a new form, would not be forgotten. In February 1945, before the war ended, the first Commonwealth Broadcasting Conference had assembled at Broadcasting House in London to exchange views on a wide range of subjects, and delegates had television demonstrated to them at Alexandra Palace.

Sir Ian Jacob, BBC Director-General 1952-59

As a result of subsequent meetings the Conference evolved into the Commonwealth Broadcasting Association (CBA), set up in 1974. It still has a Secretariat in London and over 50 Commonwealth countries are members.

Similar moves were occurring in Europe where there had been a union of broadcasters since 1926. The war disrupted its work and the rump of the organisation came under Nazi German control, following the withdrawal of Allied countries. In 1950 a conference was convened by the BBC in Torquay and the European Broadcasting Union (EBU) was set up anew with Sir Ian Jacob, then Director of Overseas Services, as President. He later became the BBC's Director-General. The work of both the CBA and EBU, linking British broadcasters with those in other countries, was to have great significance in the near future. For example, in June/July 1954, following four years' work, there was an exchange of television programmes between eight European countries, including Britain, under an arrangement called Eurovision.

Meanwhile Sir William Haley and the senior managers of the Overseas and European Service Divisions were grappling with the problem of the future shape and size of these operations. They had grown enormously during the war and now took up something like one-third of the total cost of BBC broadcasting along with one-sixth of the staff. Forty-four languages, including English, were noted by the Beveridge Committee in 1950, with the weekly hours of broadcasting standing at about 669 compared with 375 at home. The licence fee was quite inadequate to cover all this and a separate grant-in-aid had been arranged during the war, drawn from general taxation, to pay for overseas broadcasts. Various Government departments, including the Foreign Office and Commonwealth Relations Office, prescribed the countries to which broadcasts should be directed together with the hours of broadcasting, but editorial responsibility was left with the BBC. Were there now to be cuts and/or additions to the list of receiving countries? How was the BBC to cope with the staff changes involved? What was badly needed was some sense of stability and continuity. This was some time away, and BBC managers were frequently in despair as, no doubt, were those in Government responsible for implementing savings in a war-shattered economy.

While there were additions to services overall, large reductions were made against a background of protests from a wide range of people, including politicans of all parties. The changes that did occur reflected, often crudely, the fluid political situation. So, for example, with relationships easing, the Russian Service re-started in March 1946 after an absence of three years and Soviet delegates visited the BBC in 1947. But the continuation of this service presented problems as the Cold War developed in 1948 and 1949, and jamming became more widespread and efficient. Other additions were services in Urdu, Hebrew and Indonesian in 1949. There were reductions in the scale of European language services in 1945, and the elimination of those to Belgium and Luxembourg in 1952. Comprehensive reductions had been made in 1951, largely due to the Chancellor of the Exchequer, Hugh Gaitskell, who was no lover of what had collectively been called the External Services since 1948. He cited the increased costs of the Korean War as a major factor in his decision. To him the External Services, European and Overseas, were 'frills'.

Sir Ian Jacob called for a proper and thorough review. Under pressure, the Conservative Government relented in July 1952 with the announcement of the setting up of a Committee under Lord Drogheda which reported in April 1954. Its remit was a wide one, 'to assess the value of the overseas information services', which included the BBC and agencies such as the British Council, and to recommend future policy. The Report, not published in full at the time, was unsatisfactory from many points of view, particularly in its belief that the need was, primarily, to appeal to the influential listeners abroad and to use services such as those offered by the BBC as tactical rather than strategic, long-term weapons. This was to prove a particularly unfortunate attitude as the crises of the Soviet invasion of Hungary and Suez, both in 1956, proved. Like many Reports, Lord Drogheda's had settled very little. The 1951 Beveridge Report, covering the whole field of home and external broadcasting, had been almost equally inconclusive in some important aspects of this fast-moving world, but, generally, found in favour of the BBC's efforts.

68

Home-made television set constructed from a Second
World War airborne radar receiver, 1948

Front and rear view of the 'Green
Screen Wonder' – a home-built
television set, 1948

1949 Receiving Licence

Bush television set from the early Fifties

An Emitron camera used from
1937 until the early Fifties

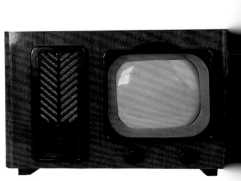

First postwar Pye television set, 1946

Beveridge Report

Lord Beveridge brought to the task of chairing this sixth major investigation into British broadcasting prodigious gifts and much public esteem, the latter largely due to his contribution to the setting up of what was, increasingly, to be called the 'welfare state'. He was a liberal not a socialist, had a deep sense of public duty, disliked monopolies and favoured a free but regulated market. With a distinguished academic background, he viewed the BBC as a kind of popular university.

It was remarked at the time by the liberal newspaper, the *News Chronicle*, that 'A Question Mark' hung over the BBC. Few of the members of the Committee knew much about broadcasting but there was a good political mix, and some well-known names such as Lady Megan Lloyd George and Selwyn Lloyd. The latter, a Conservative MP, whose minority report was to be of the utmost significance in determining the breaking of the BBC's broadcasting monopoly, later became Foreign Secretary. The Committee researched far and wide, receiving a very large number of letters and 223 memoranda from a huge range of individuals and organisations. Visits to America persuaded one member, Alderman Reeves, a Labour MP, that British television was best and that 'advertising matter' was 'obtrusive and objectionable'. Selwyn Lloyd agreed but felt that advertising in British broadcasting could be handled differently, and he was, in due course, proved to be correct.

The BBC managers and officials concerned with writing the BBC's evidence to the Committee ('one witness among others', as Beveridge remarked) worked long and diligently. A 10-year capital development plan and financial forecasts were supplied along with a plea that the Corporation should retain the whole of the licence fee income. The BBC at that time received 85% of the net licence revenue, with part of the other 15% deducted for the cost of collecting it. Haley argued strongly for the continuation of the monopoly on the grounds of the 'responsibilities to the community' required from broadcasting: competition would lead to the bad driving out the good. In accordance, presumably, with Haley's priorities, television got far less attention than radio, demonstrating

Selwyn Lloyd MP: A member of the Beveridge Committee

once again how even those closest to the action are frequently guilty of failing to see the whole game.

The Committee's findings showed, conclusively, how well-organised evidence can change minds; any idea the members may have had of breaking up the BBC or introducing competition was dropped. In the final Report, the BBC's programming achievements, the ultimate test, were acknowledged. The first recommendation, from which only Selwyn Lloyd dissented, was that the BBC, after the expiry of its current licence in 1952, 'should be continued as the authority responsible for all broadcasting in the United Kingdom, including Television and the Overseas Services'.

There were reservations on a number of points. The Governors should become 'masters in their own house' and their number increased from seven to nine; indeed, they should collectively be regarded in their part-time broadcasting work rather like 'a Minister in charge of a Government Department'. This last idea was not taken up by the Government, but Beveridge's strictures on the need to keep the work of the BBC's staff in touch with public opinion was an early reminder of anxiety about 'the power of the media', real or imaginary, and how this was increasingly to dominate debates on broadcasting as the television age developed. In due course, the BBC developed an administrative machinery better adapted to dealing with matters such as research, public relations and accountability.

Another of the Beveridge recommendations which reflected concerns was that Scotland, Wales and Northern Ireland should have 'National Commissions' of their own, with strong powers. 'Federalism' is not an idea of the Nineties. In practice, the BBC set up National Broadcasting Councils

for Wales and Scotland in January 1953 with Northern Ireland, for complex political reasons, having an Advisory Council. At the same time three National Governors were appointed to sit on the central Board of Governors. These chaired their own Councils which were to become increasingly significant.

Beveridge and his colleagues also showed some interest in what came to be called the 'democratisation of broadcasting'. They proposed in recommendation 64 that a 'Hyde Park of the Air' should be considered, where minorities could sound off, an idea which took 20 years more to become reality with the introduction of access programmes. Another liberating recommendation was that the ban on broadcast discussions about questions which might be debated in the House of Commons within a fortnight (the so-called '14-day rule') should be rethought. It was not until July 1957 that the issue was finally resolved, an indication of some of the restrictions under which news and current affairs operated in the early Fifties.

It fell to the Labour Government to deal with the Beveridge Report, but before it could take action on its White Paper of 10 July 1951, the Conservatives had been returned to power, led, for the last time, by Winston Churchill. Attlee and his colleagues had been prepared to accept many of Beveridge's main proposals, including the continuation of the monopoly, but on the question of finance it proposed to retain 15% of the licence fee, partly to pay for collection. While the powers of the Governors were to be strengthened, one controversial proposal was dropped. This would have involved a more 'democratic' approach in the selection of National Regional Governors and Councils than that applicable in England for the central Board of Governors.

However, the mere idea had reinforced the view that Scotland, Wales and Northern Ireland have separate identities and cannot always be assumed to take on English ways of working.

The debate which followed the publication of the White Paper revealed many cross-currents between the political parties, with widely differing views on, for example, the monopoly question, on television development and on trade unions in the BBC. On this last question the BBC had proposed the extension of joint consultation with its employees, staff associations having been set up in 1940 and 1941.

When the Labour Government fell, it lost what was to be its last chance to prevent the commercialisation of broadcasting. Fears of what social effects would ensue from such a development were widespread in both the Liberal and Conservative Parties as well as being deeply engrained in most members of the Labour Party. Events were soon to show that Reith's ideal of what he injudiciously called 'the brute force of monopoly' was no longer easily defensible. The battle was about to be joined and much of what the Beveridge Committee (with a single exception) had argued for would be overturned. Selwyn Lloyd, who had found himself 'substantially in agreement with my colleagues on a considerable number of matters contained in their Report', wanted the BBC's monopoly to be ended and, following a vigorous campaign based partly on principle but also on self-interest, ended it was.

Ironically, it was in television that the monopoly was first broken, the medium to which Beveridge and his colleagues had given relatively little attention.

Pressures for Competition

The events that followed are generally regarded as a dramatic illustration that power can be exerted by intense and well-organised political lobbying. Shortly after the fall of the Labour Government, a Conservative Party parliamentary committee, the Broadcasting Study Group, was set up. It issued its own Report on the future of British broadcasting in February 1952, three months before the Government issued its first White Paper. An intense struggle raged within the party between supporters of the BBC and those, including the members of the Study Group, who wanted change.

The White Paper, while praising the BBC, made the first brief and tentative suggestion for breaking the monopoly. This was a subject, it said, which 'had much exercised the minds of all those who had considered it'. Clause 7 was the crucial one, for here it was proposed that 'some element of competition' should be permitted 'in the expanding field of television', when more resources were available. Radio was to be left with the BBC.

This went too far for many in all parties, but not nearly far enough for others. The debate became intense both inside and outside Parliament with passions often running high, the House of Lords being the arena in which some of the fiercest skirmishes took place. In a 10-day debate in the Lords in May 1952, over half the speakers were critical of the Government, but Lord Woolton, Lord Privy Seal and the man in charge of broadcasting policy, was, ironically, helped by an intemperate speech from Reith, who had been created a Baron in 1940. Reith talked of selling the BBC heritage 'down the river', of 'compromise and expediency' and of 'betrayal and surrender'.

The introduction into the country of sponsored broadcasts was compared with the introduction of dog-racing into England and the coming of the Black Death.

Lord Hailsham, who was also opposed to his party's plans, made more interesting points, thus illustrating the complexities of the argument from the Conservative point of view. Since, in the act of sponsorship, the consumer buys nothing directly, this 'is not, in the ordinary sense, private enterprise' and 'the BBC is not a monopoly in any accepted sense of the word, because it sells nothing'. These arguments were to become important when the actual mechanism of commercial (or its preferred name 'Independent') television was eventually set up. In the House of Commons, however, where the debate took place in June 1952, the younger and more business-oriented Tories pressed for change. Even in the business world, there were intriguing anomalies, with press interests at first opposed to commercial television because of the possible effect on their own advertising revenue. This philosophy of 'competition yes, so long as I am not affected' was to be revised when it became clear that big profits could be made from the new system and that the advertising pool could be enlarged. Despite his coolness towards the BBC and his feeling that broadcasting policy was a low priority, Sir Winston Churchill did not support the commercial television proposal. 'Why do we need this peep-show?' he asked.

The battle moved away from Parliament as the Government pondered its next move and two new national organisations were set up to support the opposing camps. On 18 June 1953 the National Television Council was formed to fight the introduction of commercial television with Lady Violet Bonham-Carter, a Liberal, as Chairman and Labour MP Christopher Mayhew as chief organiser. A month later, the Popular Television Association, presided over by the Earl of Derby, came into being to warn the public of the dangers of monopoly. Its diverse membership included Rex Harrison, Alec Bedser, Somerset Maugham, Malcolm Muggeridge and A.J.P.Taylor. A key question asked by this group was 'Why should broadcasting be treated differently from the Press?'

The BBC's position was delicate for, as usual, it did not wish to be identified with the view of particular political parties. The Labour Party also had problems. While most of its members regarded the notion of commercial broadcasting as vulgar and a possible propaganda tool for a market economy based on free enterprise, it slowly came to realise that the proposed new channel might be popular. After all, the effects of competition from such stations as Radio Luxembourg had been there for all to see.

After much argument and hard thinking, the Government made public its plans in November 1953 and a Television Bill was published in March of the following year. It was an ingenious compromise which allowed the setting up of commercial television stations owned by private companies but, under a new public corporation, to be called the Independent Television Authority. This Authority would own new transmitters, which it would hire out to the companies, and it would have considerable powers in controlling their programme output. Revenue from selling advertising time would provide the companies with an income – sponsorship was not admissible. This new structure, a controlled mix of the American commercial system and the British system, was, in 1955, to become the second arm of the broadcasting duopoly. The BBC now had a fight on its hands, but it had not been idle in the closing years of its monopoly.

Strong on Both Wings

The Goon Show gang (from left): Peter Sellers, Harry Secombe, Spike Milligan, Michael Bentine

This was a phrase used by Sir Ian Jacob when he addressed the BBC's senior staff at an internal liaison meeting in October 1955. In his pep-talk, he took pains to assure his colleagues that, in the Government's words, the BBC remained 'the main instrument for broadcasting in the UK'. He emphasised that those working in radio should not think of themselves as 'the Forgotten Army... No greater illusion can be fostered than that sound broadcasting is a spent force or that it's likely to become one in our time'. This was a wise observation both from the point of view of the national interest but also from the narrower, tactical, BBC one. Yet it set him and his managers, Sir George Barnes, the Director of Television Broadcasting, and Sir Lindsay Wellington, the Director of Sound Broadcasting, formidable planning problems. In 1954-55 the BBC's expenditure on radio, about £10 million, was double that spent on television but within three years the two were running roughly equal at £11 million. As competition in television grew, the gap widened dramatically at the expense of radio. The selection of priorities was ever more urgent.

Jacob, an early and enthusiastic supporter of planning within large organisations, had recognised the increasingly competitive nature of broadcasting. In 1953 he had announced a general 10-year plan, with an additional five-year plan for television. These envisaged ambitious developments in both radio and television as well as in capital projects involving engineering. The BBC was constrained, unlike private companies, in the matter of raising loans, the licence fee being fixed by the Government (at £3, in 1954, for a combined radio and television licence). The Government also controlled wavelengths and needed to decide which colour system to adopt, a complex technical problem involving international sensitivities. As a result, many of the target dates set by the BBC plans were severely delayed, with colour television coming in 1967/68 instead of 1956/57 and a second BBC television channel in 1964/65 instead of 1957/58.

One of radio's most popular shows, *Hancock's Half-Hour*, later transferred to television

The *What's My Line?* panel quiz a challenger, under Eamonn Andrews' chairmanship

This Is Your Life: Eamonn Andrews with guest Vera Lynn in October 1957

There were, nevertheless, some remarkably successful programmes in the last days of the monopoly, both on radio and television. Many of these lasted for years and laid down new areas of interest, new approaches to entertainment and new attitudes towards the treatment of public issues.

In radio entertainment the most innovative programme series of the period was *The Goon Show*, operating under this name from June 1952, having originally been called *Crazy People*. Its surreal characters, seemingly chaotic format and dialogue, supremely imaginative puns and double-entendres continued to delight audiences into the Sixties, with many repeats after that. Spike Milligan was the architect of the show and one of the group of zany performers which

What Do You Know?: a weekly paper-and-pencil quiz game in Northern Ireland had Irish international rugby player Ernest Strathdee (left) as question master

included Peter Sellers, Harry Secombe and, for a time, Michael Bentine. The style of humour created by The Goons was fundamentally to influence much of broadcast humour in the future. *Pick of the Pops* began on the Light Programme in 1955, heralding a new style of music popular among younger audiences. It, and successor programmes, relied on the skills of disc-jockeys. Other popular radio programmes of the early Fifties were *Hancock's Half-Hour*, *Friday Night Is Music Night* and *What Do You Know?*, which evolved into *Brain of Britain* in the late Sixties, with Robert Robinson as the quiz-master. For more serious listeners, June 1954 saw the transmission of one of the most famous of all feature programmes, Dylan Thomas's *Under Milk Wood*, and the first of Antony Hopkins's long-running series, *Talking About Music*. In 1955 *From Our Own Correspondent*, half-hour talks from BBC correspondents around the world, also began its long run. Classical music continued to attract large audiences, despite the growth of LP record sales. The Proms flourished under a new baton, that of the dynamic and popular Sir Malcolm Sargent, who was criticised by some for being unsympathetic to much contemporary music.

The Quatermass Experiment: Television's first successful science fiction series

The 'Big Brother' poster (alias designer Roy Oxley) used in Rudolph Cartier's production of George Orwell's *Nineteen Eighty Four*

with the Lyons brought together Ben Lyon and his wife Bebe Daniels and their grown-up children Richard and Barbara

Television had an easier task in moving into new areas since there was still so much new ground to explore in that medium. In drama, *The Quatermass Experiment* (the first successful science-fiction series) and a dramatisation of George Orwell's novel *Nineteen Eighty Four* both caused sensations, while *The Grove Family* became the first television family serial to attract the sort of attention expected by *The Archers* on radio. *Dixon of Dock Green* was the earliest successful police series. New quiz and panel game formats were explored in

What's My Line? and *Animal, Vegetable, Mineral?* These shows helped to create television personalities such as Gilbert Harding, Lady Barnett and Sir Mortimer Wheeler, while David Attenborough began his long line of highly successful natural history series with *Zoo Quest* in 1954. Two of the longest-running BBC current events programmes began in 1953 and 1954, namely *Panorama* and *Sportsview*, both of which had a profound effect on future broadcasting in their respective areas.

The Grove Family: First television family serial to attract a mass audience

For children, the period introduced *All Your Own* presented by Huw Wheldon, later Managing Director Television, *Bill and Ben the Flowerpot Men*, *For Deaf Children* (later called *Vision On*), *Crackerjack* and *The Woodentops*, while notable variety and comedy entertainment offerings included *The Good Old Days* and *Life with the Lyons*. The latter series transferred from radio. Shortly before Independent Television, or ITV as it came to be called, opened on 22 September 1955, the BBC screened for the first time *This Is Your Life*, an idea which came from America. This was an enormous success, which much later transferred to the competitor, an early example of one way in which the two television services were to relate to each other, by competing yet feeding off each other in programme terms. In a similar way, radio was to become a testing ground for much good television writing and performing.

Bill and Ben: TV puppets which attracted large children's audiences

Facing the Competitor

'The Competitor' was the name of an internal BBC document with a circulation restricted to senior executives. It was designed to give as many details as possible about ITV plans, programmes and schedules to those in the BBC engaged in offering alternatives. To some BBC staff, the atmosphere created by this new competitive situation seemed senselessly confrontational. Was the idea to turn broadcasting into a kind of war zone, complete with spying, ambitions to 'beat the other side' and even the achievement of victory over the enemy? Was this the best way to serve the public and was it going to be easy to adapt from more 'gentlemanly' ways?

It took some time for these questions to be answered, but there were clear signs of how the situation would develop in the early months of the duopoly when on 22 September 1955 the BBC – and BBC Radio at that – succeeded in scooping many of the headlines on the opening night of the new independent commercial channel. The following morning's popular press gave more space to the death of Grace Archer in *The Archers* on the Light Programme than to the start of ITV. Audience comparisons are unfair here since relatively few people could receive the new television programmes, but for the five-year-old radio series to achieve an audience of 8 million on such an occasion was remarkable. This gesture of defiance towards ITV can only be understood if it is remembered that BBC Radio staff, seeing the rising costs of television, were concerned to show that their medium still had life in it. The enemy in their case was television, not just ITV. The episode showed that if the coming battle was to be tough, then the BBC was prepared to fight hard.

The hours of television broadcasting permitted by the Post Office were increased in 1955 from 41 to 50, with the evening beginning at 7pm instead of 7.30pm. This was good news for the viewer and for ITV companies which could increase their income from the extra advertising available. But increases in transmission hours would always be a mixed blessing for the BBC where income could not rise except when licence numbers were growing. At the same time, reliable audience research became vitally important so that audience sizes could be measured and views on programmes analysed to ensure how best to use the programme money available. For the ITV companies, audience size was, and remains, much the most important factor, since advertising revenue depends on it.

As the regional companies joined the expanding independent network, more people were able to see this new style of programming with its bright and breezy commercials offering, in the middle of a boom, an attractive lifestyle full of consumer goods. Prime Minister Macmillan observed in 1957: 'Our people have never had it so good'. The sentiment symbolised the era.

By August 1958, 80% of the population could receive ITV and the BBC's share of the audience had dropped. The lowest point was reached at the end of 1957 when, according to BBC estimates, the Corporation's share of the audience capable of receiving both television channels was only 28%. Radio audiences were also falling. ITV's audience research painted an even more depressing picture for the BBC, a fact which added pressure for a common system of measurement. Attempts were made to achieve this in 1954, but success did not come until 1981.

From 1955, audience research by BBC and ITV and by academic and other bodies became increasingly important. Inside the BBC, managers agonised over what an acceptable audience was. Some thought quality was more important than quantity while others realised that economics and politics dictated that nothing less than a 50:50 split, averaged over time, would do.

The death of Grace Archer (actress Ysanne Churchman) in *The Archers* took press attention away from ITV's opening night

Whack-O! made Jimmy Edwards into a
major television star

1968: Sir Hugh Greene, arguably the second
most famous Director-General of the BBC

The Black and White Minstrel Show: One of
the period's favourite musical entertainments

Children's favourites: The piglets *Pinky and Perky*

Another important problem for the BBC was that staff were being attracted away by the higher salaries offered by ITV, and within six months in 1955/6 about 500 left. Fortunately, the Corporation had an effective training scheme and lost staff were quickly replaced. When writers, artists and other programme contributors, too, found themselves in a competitive market, their fees tended to go up. Competition, far from reducing the cost of television, was increasing it. On a relatively fixed income, that was hard, but the companies, which had lost money in the early days of ITV, now began to make it in abundance. By 1960, ITV had more to spend on television than the BBC.

But after the first shaky two years of duopoly, BBC managers, producers and schedulers began a successful fightback, without compromising serious programmes. There was a determination to avoid going down the path of 'easy'

American-style programming, using quiz shows and Westerns to attract big audiences without offering something more substantial. Indeed, between 1955 and 1957, the proportion of more serious BBC programmes actually increased. By 1960, when Hugh Carleton Greene took over from Sir Ian Jacob as Director-General, a firm foundation had been laid for the future when the battle for audiences would intensify.

Satisfying the growing youth audience:
Juke Box Jury, chaired by David Jacobs

Among the notable successes in the area of pure comedy entertainment were *Hancock's Half-Hour* and *Whack-O!*, which made Tony Hancock and Jimmy Edwards into major television stars.

Actor Jon Pertwee tries his hand at skiffle in *Six-Five Special*. Among the skifflers behind him, Adam Faith

David Coleman presents *Grandstand*

1967: Presenters John Noakes, Christopher Trace and Valerie Singleton sort through entries for a *Blue Peter* poster competition

Billy Cotton and The Silhouettes rehearse a number for *The Billy Cotton Band Show*

The first had begun on radio in 1954 and moved to live television in 1956. In 1959, it became one of the first series to employ a new system of electronic recording and cassette versions of some of the episodes such as *The Radio Ham* remain classics. Jimmy Edwards, the star of *Whack-O!* played a headmaster, the so-called 'Professor', in an eccentric school. It was in the tradition of Billy Bunter, which had also been adapted for television by its author Frank Richards in 1952. These innovative comedy series, whose style and format have been copied many times since, were being seen alongside a rich selection of musical entertainments, including *The Billy Cotton Band Show*, *The Eurovision Song Contest*, *The Black and White Minstrel Show* and, to satisfy the growing youth audience, *Six-Five Special* and *Juke Box Jury.* Sport, too, began to gather big audiences with new initiatives such as the first televising of the Winter Olympics from Cortina in 1956 and the start of

Grandstand two years later which, with increasingly large audiences, caused great consternation at ITV.

Children's programmes were particularly strong and innovative between 1956 and 1960 with *Lenny the Lion, Pinky and Perky* and, above all, *Blue Peter* which started in 1958 and is still very popular. It came at a time when children's programmes were fighting hard to attract audiences against ITV's competition, and it was triumphant, not only in getting more viewers, but also in its commitment to the encouragement of 'active' viewing. Its appeals for help for the needy became extremely successful.

Ventriloquist Terry Hall with *Lenny the Lion*

Rupert Davies in *Maigret,* a popular and critical success

A new department was set up to provide television programmes for schools and began transmissions in 1957. Television, along with associated publications, quickly became a valuable teaching tool and within 10 years was being viewed in 12,000 schools.

There were many serious, innovative programmes in this period: *The Sky at Night, Monitor,* the first successful arts programme, *Your Life in Their Hands,* which began a new style of medical programming, and *Face to Face,* interviews in depth with the famous conducted by John Freeman. Great drama successes were *An Age of Kings* (a Shakespeare sequence) and the first television dramatisation of the *Maigret* detective stories by Simenon.

Radio, too, started a host of long-running series such as *My Word,* an early panel game which later transferred to television, *Does the Team Think?,* a farcical, largely unscripted version of more serious discussions featuring comic performers like Jimmy Edwards, Ted Ray and Arthur Askey, *Beyond Our Ken* with Kenneth Williams and Kenneth Horne, and *Saturday Night on the Light. In Touch* was the first national radio series for the blind.

Does the Team Think?: Jimmy Wheeler, David Tomlinson, Jimmy Edwards and David Nixon (seated)

Today on radio and *Tonight* on television both began in 1957. Their titles neatly illustrate the way in which, at this time, radio was perceived as a strong medium for attracting daytime audiences, leaving the evening largely to television. Both were news and current affairs programmes of a fresh kind with, inevitably, a significant political content. Politics in the widest sense were from now on to take a more central role in the broadcast arena, and styles of dealing with politics and politicians changed in ways that had long-term implications.

A youthful Patrick Moore introduces *The Sky at Night* in 1961

Radio panel game *My Word* later transferred to television

Politics at Home and Abroad

A BBC camera looks through a teaching lens to record a delicate ear operation for the innovative series *Your Life in Their Hands*

Kenneth Horne and cast rehearsing for *Beyond Our Ken*

The Suez crisis of 1956 became the most significant event for domestic politics. Not only did it end with the downfall of Anthony Eden through ill-health and his replacement by Harold Macmillan, but it set up a tension between the Government and the BBC which itself turned into a crisis. Both the Home and External Services were involved. This crisis was a particularly vivid example of how politics and broadcasting developed a complex and interwoven relationship after the resurgence of television from 1955. On radio and television, many new ways of reporting and discussing politics sprang from this new relationship and in the process broadcasters and politicians became dependent on, but wary of, each other. Today this love-hate relationship continues, particularly at the time of General Elections.

In the Fifties, the External Services had suffered severe reductions. The Drogheda Report had threatened more cuts but, luckily, these were not applied. Nevertheless, Ian Jacob's successor in the re-named post of Director of External Broadcasting, J.B.Clark, was disturbed by the financial situation that faced him and by the Government policies that underpinned it. One of his predecessors, the first Director of the Empire Service, dared to ask which was more important, Home or External Broadcasting. This became a painfully brutal question as events developed in Egypt.

In July 1956, President Nasser nationalised the Anglo-French controlled Suez Canal Company. This resulted in frenzied diplomatic activity, followed in October by an Israeli attack across the Sinai Desert and, as it later emerged, a co-ordinated attack by British and French forces in Egypt. By early November these forces were in control of the Canal and it might have seemed the matter was settled. But there was disagreement both abroad and at home. The UN, and the USA in particular, was displeased at what was seen to be a precipitate response to the admittedly naked seizure of Anglo-French assets. At home, the opposition Labour Party began to ask questions and the nation was clearly divided.

The BBC found itself in a new position and, in particular, had to decide whether or not the Leader of the Opposition, Hugh Gaitskell, should have the right to reply to a Ministerial Broadcast by the Prime Minister, Anthony Eden. In the event he was granted radio and television broadcasts on the authority of the BBC Chairman Sir Alexander Cadogan, well known to be a Conservative, a friend and ex-colleague of Eden's at the Foreign Office and a Director of the Suez Canal Company. The Eden and Gaitskell broadcasts raised the political temperature since they were heard in the Middle East by British troops and later in translation by local listeners to the BBC Arabic service.

This episode and others convinced the Government that the BBC was not serving its interests in the way it should, and by implication, those of the country. Threats were made to cut the External Services' grant-in-aid by £1 million and a 'liaison officer' was installed in Bush House. Eventually, the calmer approach of the Lord Privy Seal, R.A.Butler, rescinded the proposed cuts. But an important point had been made, and the BBC had probably come nearer than at any time in its history to seeing the 'reserve powers' existing in its Licence and Agreement being used to impose direct Government control. International pressures resulted in the operations in Egypt being curtailed and the Anglo-French forces had to back down. Divisions not only in the country but also in the Government, along with Eden's illness, led to the Prime Minister's resignation and his replacement by Harold Macmillan in January 1957.

There was much bad-tempered debate in Parliament, in the newspapers and among the public, but the BBC Board of Governors strongly supported their managers and editors, agreeing they had acted well 'during a period of great

difficulty' which, at the same time, had included the reporting of the Soviet invasion of Hungary. It is now generally accepted that the BBC's independent role in the Suez crisis was an honourable one in the sense that it told the truth in so far as war allows. In practice, financial pressures on the BBC continued and reductions took place, particularly in the European Services.

At home, developments in reporting politics during the late Fifties took more varied, less contentious but often more interesting forms. The most important issue to be resolved after a clash of opinions was that of the so-called '14-day rule'. This had its origins in wartime and was a self-denying rule by which the Director-General William Haley, on behalf of the BBC, undertook not to broadcast any discussions on issues due to be debated in either the House of Lords or the House of Commons during a period of two weeks before such debates. It had Coalition Government support, but became increasingly difficult to justify in peacetime when the parties returned to more vigorous debating. During one broadcast of an important current affairs series, *In the News*, transmitted in February 1955, a group of four MPs from all the main parties openly protested against the so-called rule. Within months, the BBC told Charles Hill, then the Postmaster-General, that it would continue following its own rule only if the Government made it an official proscription. It did this two weeks later, requiring both the BBC and ITV to observe the rule. Most people could not see why broadcasting should be treated differently from the press and within months Ian Jacob, supported by the ITA, succeeded in getting the rule dropped for an experimental period. In July 1957 Harold Macmillan finally suspended it.

Politicians, and Ministers in particular, wanted to use radio and television to their own advantage. The *Week in Westminster*, a relatively straightforward backbench account of happenings in Parliament, had been acceptable since it started in 1929, as had *Today in Parliament*, begun in 1945. But even these programmes were regarded with suspicion by some stuffier MPs.

In 1956, Anthony Eden made the first television ministerial broadcast. This was followed in 1958 by the first appearance of a Prime Minister, Harold Macmillan, in a regular television series, *Press Conference*. A year later, Macmillan, who took a more relaxed attitude towards broadcasting than many Ministers, achieved another first when he was televised from Downing Street in informal discussion with President Eisenhower. This occurred just two months before the Prime Minister won a big majority in the first General Election that was covered on news programmes by both the BBC and ITV. The Labour Party's election broadcasts on this occasion were in a style which imitated the *Tonight* programme. Granada had already broken through restrictions about covering elections on television with their broadcasts from the Rochdale by-election in February 1958.

There were some significant political programme initiatives between 1955 and 1968, the most innovative being the start of *Highlight* on the same day that ITV began transmitting. This was a nightly programme of interviews for which Alasdair Milne, a future Director-General, and Donald Baverstock were responsible. This highly original pair in 1957 created *Tonight,* the first major topical programme to be seen on television five nights a week. Originally it was designed to fill the period between 6pm and 7pm, which had formerly been left empty so that children could be put to bed (the so-called 'Toddler's Truce'), but it soon became highly popular and achieved an audience of 5 million within a year. Its style was accessible, its pace rapid and its attitude irreverent. For this reason, and because of the strand of satirical programmes it engendered such as *That Was the Week That Was*, *Tonight* and programmes like it were often disliked by those in authority. Hugh Carleton Greene, who became Director-General in 1960, was closely identified with the new mood but quickly had to turn his attention to yet another Government Committee of Inquiry.

Director-General Hugh Carleton Greene welcomes Lord Reith at the BBC Television Service's 25th anniversary dinner

A member of the 'refreshingly different' Pilkington Committee: Entertainer Joyce Grenfell

Philip Harben: One of the first to make cookery popular on television

Marconi 'coffin' camera used in the BBC colour experiments at Alexandra Palace

Pilkington Approves

The Committee on Broadcasting, chaired by Sir Harry Pilkington, a successful businessman, was set up by the Macmillan Government in July 1960, less than a year after the General Election of 1959. It began work in August and reported in June 1962. Its remit was wide, but excluded consideration of the future of the External Services which, it was assumed, would remain the responsibility of the BBC. The future of both the ITA and the BBC was taken for granted, but their finances, constitutions and structures were to be investigated.

As with every Committee of this kind, the choice of members was crucial. In this case the hand of Macmillan was clearly visible, and Hugh Carleton Greene felt that the Prime Minister 'was sensitive to the wind of change in broadcasting as in other fields'. He was referring to a speech made by Macmillan to the South African Parliament in February 1960 on the new climate in Africa. The membership of the Committee was refreshingly different from that of Beveridge. It included a radio research engineer; a footballer, Billy Wright; the entertainer Joyce Grenfell; the literary critic and author Richard Hoggart; and a headmaster, a trade unionist and businessmen.

The BBC took great care with the preparation of evidence in support of its programme record and with its case for expansion. Among its objectives were the need to expand both its sound and television services, to introduce colour television, and local radio on VHF, to secure a second television channel and to introduce stereo radio. Above all, it wanted the licence fee to be retained and not have advertising forced on it. It also wanted the existing £4 combined television and radio licence to be increased to £5. For the first time, there was a realisation that for some people this seemingly modest sum, equivalent to the cost of a few packets of cigarettes a week, might be viewed more warmly if it could be paid by instalments.

In 1962, the Government solved the problem of financing the BBC by keeping the licence fee at £4 but releasing the BBC from paying £1 of this in excise duty. The proposal that old-age pensioners and any other groups in society should qualify for a reduced rate of licence fee was firmly rejected. Recognising that comparisons were dangerous, the Committee printed in its Report a 'league table' of licence fees in Europe, which showed the United Kingdom's as the cheapest, especially when the excise duty was accounted for. The British public appeared to be getting very good value for money.

Internal discussions among BBC programme-makers during the preparation of papers for Pilkington uncovered some interesting views. Many thought the BBC and the audience had benefited from competition, and Greene himself later agreed that he did not regret the ending of the monopoly. Others felt that standards had fallen and although it was never easy to define what standards meant in a society changing so speedily, the question focused on whether or not there was a decline in the number of serious programmes. These, according to BBC evidence, included news and current affairs, documentaries, talks and discussions, opera, ballet and serious music. Drama was a more ambiguous programme category, and more difficult to classify.

Donald Houston (the narrator) and Catherine Dolan (Rosie Probert) in a 1957 adaptation of Dylan Thomas' *Under Milk Wood*

In figures submitted to the Committee, the BBC showed how the proportion of such serious programmes transmitted in peak viewing hours (7pm to 10.30pm) had declined slightly between 1958 and 1960, but remained at roughly one-third, the figure set by Corporation policy. The Committee noted how it would be easier for that figure to be maintained if a second channel were available to the BBC and was more concerned with what it repeatedly referred to as 'triviality', particularly on ITV.

In its concept of 'People's Television', the ITA had severe reservations about the BBC's definition of 'serious' programmes and did not wish their measurement within peak hours to be emphasised. Pilkington found much of the independent channel's output 'trivial and shoddy'. There was also concern about violence in many programmes, about aspects of advertisements and about the balance of programming in satisfying 'the varied and many-sided tastes of the public'. In a damning and what many people thought was an exaggerated sentence the Committee wrote: 'We conclude that the dissatisfaction

camera closes in on a scene from Henry V in the series *An Age of Kings*, a cycle of Shakespeare's historical plays

Mary Whitehouse, founder of the National Viewers' and Listeners' Association

Among the celebrities at a reception to celebrate the opening of the new Television Centre on 29 June 1960: Comedy stars Sidney James, Hattie Jacques and Eric Sykes

with television can be ascribed to the independent television service'. From now on, the whole question of the social effects of television was to come under closer scrutiny, with issues such as the portrayal of violence, sexual explicitness and bad language being researched and written about in detail. Two landmarks were the Himmelweit Report ('Television and the Child') of 1958, which the BBC and ITV considered carefully, and the founding of a pressure group, the National Viewers' and Listeners' Association in 1965, following campaigns by Mrs Mary Whitehouse, an ex-schoolteacher who felt passionately about the social consequences of more permissive television. Some observers, while not necessarily agreeing with Mrs Whitehouse, felt that ITV dealt more intelligently with the 'clean-up TV' campaign than the BBC, which tended to ignore its critics' sometimes skilful manoeuvrings.

Pilkington and his Committee had in general endorsed the BBC and hardly criticised radio, but many ITV managers were incensed by what they saw as the unfairness of the Report and the abrasiveness of its tone. It was deemed priggish and too concerned with the views of élites and special-interest groups. The stress placed on 'professionalism in the BBC', a concept which received much attention in the coming years, suggested self-satisfaction. For its part, the BBC was riding high with the new Television Centre, described as 'the world's largest television factory', opening at White City in west London on 29 June 1960.

Two White Papers were issued in 1962 and they gave some indication of what the future held. The BBC, which was to stay 'the main instrument of broadcasting in the UK', was authorised to start a second television service and to increase its hours of sound broadcasting. But, as with many Government committee reports, not all of Pilkington's recommendations had been accepted. The question of the BBC's finances was not addressed. Local radio was not given the go-ahead, (and the BBC waited three more years for a decision). ITV was not to be restructured and disciplined as had been suggested, but neither was it given a second channel.

It would be wrong to think that, because many of its recommendations were not taken up, the work of the Pilkington Committee was largely wasted. It drew

Television Centre

Television Centre was built in the Fifties on a 13-acre site in Shepherds Bush, west London, which had been home in 1908 for part of the Franco-British Exhibition. This took place four years after the signing of the Entente Cordiale when relations between the two countries were at their best. In the same year, an exceptional Olympic Games meeting was held in the nearby White City Stadium, now the site of the BBC's newest building.

Although the designs for Television Centre were accepted by the BBC's Board of Governors in March 1950, work was held up by Government limitations on capital expenditure and there was a part standstill until the end of 1953. One advantage of the delay was that the plans were reshaped to take account of world advances in television.

Work on the main seven-storey block, covering 3.5 acres, nearly twice the area covered by St Paul's, began in 1956. The first of the new major studios, seven in all at first, was brought into operation on the day of the official opening, 29 June 1960. The circular centre court of the main office block was dominated by a fountain with an obelisk 40 feet high, surmounted by a gilded bronze figure of Helios, the all-seeing Sun god of Greek mythology. The studios were arranged in the shape of a letter C around the centre circular block, allowing scenery to be transported into the studios from a service road around the edge. Radiating from the main block were the scenery block, a restaurant block and the East Tower, which accommodated film handling as well as engineering and house-service workshops and stores.

Many changes and additions have been made to the building, notably the addition of a 'spur' which changed the aerial configuration of the building into the shape of a number '9' or a question mark. In 1969, BBC Television News moved from Alexandra Palace into this 'spur'.

attention to important questions concerned with institutional structures and professional attitudes in broadcasting, to questions of finance and control and to growing concerns about whether broadcasting and, in particular, television was having undesirable social effects. In retrospect, it is easy to accuse some of those in charge at the BBC of being too complacent about all of these issues but, at the time, there were more pressing questions. In particular, how, in an increasingly competitive climate and with limited finance, was the Corporation to continue to make more good, new, varied programmes? How was it to keep in contact with the public mood? Was it to lead or reflect or both? Hugh Carleton Greene as Director-General seemed to have the right qualifications of optimism, energy and ebullience to lead the team which would have to answer these questions.

Greene Light

Following the Pilkington Report, the BBC was in a triumphant mood and Hugh Carleton Greene was the real and symbolic leader who helped to create it. He remained Director-General for just over nine years, during which time success and crisis followed each other in what seem, in retrospect, an exceptional fashion. Many judged Greene to be the man who pulled and pushed the BBC through its most successful decade. Others think he was fortunate to have served in the highest office at a time when money was reasonably plentiful, the country was determined to experiment and enjoy itself and there was a plentiful supply of able men and women anxious to achieve success in an expanding industry. The BBC, in this period of 'the swinging Sixties' and 'the pendulum years' – both images expressing change and alternation – was a place for the bright and the young to be in. The general traineeship scheme, which the BBC instituted in the mid-Fifties, was extremely popular with brighter university graduates and many future managers and producers came into the Corporation through this route.

When Greene became Director-General in January 1960, there were about 10 million combined radio and television licences and over 17,000 staff. In 1969, when Charles Curran took over in much more difficult economic times, there were over 16 million licences and nearly 24,000 staff. The price of the monochrome licence had increased, after delays and arguments, from £4 to £6, with an extra £5 being charged for a colour licence, and the BBC's annual income had risen from £33 million to £80 million. Apart from the prospect of inflation, the take-up of new licences would soon level off as ownership of television became almost universal. Greene was accused, notably by Mrs Whitehouse, of having been responsible more than anyone else 'for the moral collapse which characterized the Sixties and Seventies', an opinion which now seems extreme. For his part Greene saw society changing for various reasons and felt the BBC should mirror these changes. He wanted 'the mirror to be honest, without any curves, and held with as steady a hand as may be'. He wanted to open windows and let in a little fresh air, and there is no doubt he did this with considerable glee.

Within a few years of the start of ITV, critics were accusing television in general and BBC television in particular of creating a destructive, permissive and nihilistic social climate.

Yet it is often forgotten how confrontational and non-consensual the general mood already was in the late Fifties. The influence of the American cinema had been important, with the arrival of cult figures such as James Dean in *Rebel Without a Cause* (1955) and Marlon Brando in *The Wild Ones* (1959), while the economic boom of the Fifties had spawned Teddy boys, pop culture and singers with assumed names such as Billy Fury and Marty Wilde. Youth had money in its pocket and this brought power, although the real power-holders were the entrepreneurs who exploited the situation.

Well before television entered its more open or permissive phase, depending on one's viewpoint, John Osborne's *Look Back in Anger* (1956) had appeared and the young, unknown writer Colin Wilson had written *The Outsider* (1956). Older moral codes were questioned when, in 1960, the Penguin publishers of D.H. Lawrence's *Lady Chatterley's Lover* were acquitted of the charge of obscenity. This was two years before BBC television launched the satirical show *That Was the Week That Was* — to the surprise of some and the alarm of others. The arguments about whether television is a creator or reflector of social habits, even

A violent scene from Peter Watkins' *The War Game*

assuming a clear connection between viewing and behaving, are complex. But it was obvious that Greene was a questioner of authority and it is ironic that, eventually, he had to

bow to the authority of a new Chairman, Lord Hill, whom he saw as having been appointed, quite deliberately, by a Labour Prime Minister, Harold Wilson, to bring him to heel.

Meanwhile, Greene's relationship with earlier Chairmen — Sir Arthur fforde, an academic, and Lord Normanbrook, a former Secretary to the Cabinet — had generally been good. Despite differences in background and temperament, they supported him through difficult times. An early crisis was caused by a remarkable film, *The War Game,* an example of 'faction' (ie a mixture of fiction and documentary), made in 1965 by Peter Watkins, a brilliant producer who felt passionately about public ignorance of the effects of nuclear war. Made at a time when the Campaign for Nuclear Disarmament was growing in strength, the film had obvious and dramatic political implications, especially as it contained scenes of horrifying realism. After much internal debate, viewings to staff on closed-circuit and a special screening for a number of Governors and Whitehall defence advisers, Normanbrook and Greene decided that the film could not be seen publicly. It was later screened in cinemas, and eventually in the Eighties on BBC television, but at the time Watkins and many who supported him were incensed by the decision. Whatever else the incident proved, Greene emerged, censor or responsible manager, as someone who could make decisions which appeared to contradict his reputation.

Producer Jonathan Miller, left, at work on
Alice in Wonderland in 1966

After careful planning BBC2 was launched in 1964, the year of the replacement of Sir Alec Douglas-Home, Macmillan's successor, by Harold Wilson. Political pundits observed that the Conservative Prime Minister was less capable of using television to put his message across than his Labour counterpart, and henceforth image-building was to become an increasingly potent factor in elections. The BBC had mounted a big publicity campaign to launch the new channel, using the rather bizarre symbol of a kangaroo with a baby in its pouch and with the even more unlikely names of Hullabaloo and Custard. The evening of the launch on 20 April was sadly marred by a huge power failure in west London and at one point candles appeared on the screen. The Director of Television observed: 'It would be naive to suppose the new channel was launched into an entirely friendly world'. The press had a field day.

The Forsyte Saga: 18 million viewers watched the final episode

But there was now more programme choice on offer, although it took some time for the public to appreciate that the new channel was not exclusively highbrow. Apart from a wide range of educational and educative programmes, BBC2 was able to experiment with new forms of presentation, to provide minority interest programmes such as those for the deaf and offer late-night discussion programmes, the most successful being *Late Night Line-Up.* There were also popular and fresh programmes such as the situation comedy *The Likely Lads,* and the highly successful *Forsyte Saga*, which was sold around the world and attracted 18 million viewers to its last episode. For serious viewers, there was Jonathan Miller's interpretation of Plato's *Symposium* and of *Alice in Wonderland,* the arts series *Omnibus,* numerous original Ken Russell films about the lives and work of great composers such as Elgar and Richard Strauss, innovative music series such as *Masterclass,* and the science series *Horizon.* Among outstanding documentaries was the 26-part series *The Great War,* which made magnificent use of archive material and interviews with survivors.

Highly successful sitcom, *The Likely Lads*, starred Rodney Bewes and James Bolam, seen here with Dilys Watling

Artist Desmond Marwood was commissioned to draw the kangaroos Hullabaloo and Custard, the symbol which launched BBC2

Huw Wheldon, editor and presenter of the arts magazine
Monitor, who became Managing Director of BBC Television

One BBC2 series transmitted near the end of Greene's period as Director-General was *Civilisation.* This thoughtful and beautiful 13-part project, presented by Sir Kenneth Clark, art historian and former Chairman of the Independent Television Authority, took two years to make and was accompanied by a richly illustrated book. Described by Huw Wheldon, then Managing Director of BBC Television, as 'a milestone in television history', it successfully demonstrated how the medium could be used to present sustained and original ideas.

Viewers enjoyed repeats of *Dad's Army* (with Arthur Lowe, right, as the bumptious Captain Mainwaring) into the Nineties

Winning numerous prizes and selling worldwide, *Civilisation* established a new television genre; later series and books dealt with the history of scientific thought *(The Ascent of Man)*, the history of the USA *(America)* and the Royal art collection *(Royal Heritage).*

These series and others like them were classed as 'educative' and appealed to a wide general public. For those who wanted a more committed and structured approach to learning, educational series for adults had been provided on BBC television since 1963. Two years later a new department, Further Education, Television, was created to join a similar radio department to offer series, books and other back-up facilities to enable viewers to learn, for example, a foreign language, take up a hobby or update professional skills.

A milestone in television history: *Civilisation* with Sir Kenneth Clark

The years 1960-69 probably saw the start of more successful popular entertainment series than any other comparable period. Among them was *Till Death Us Do Part*, about the loud-mouthed Garnett family, which made the name of its writer Johnny Speight and its star Warren Mitchell, gaining audiences of up to 19 million despite shocking many with its bad language. Earlier, *Steptoe and Son*, about two rag-and-bone men, had begun as a single play and developed into a long-running series. With an equally unlikely subject, a group of elderly men in the Home Guard, *Dad's Army* also established itself and ran for years, with highly successful repeats as recently as 1991. *The Black and White Minstrel Show* continued to reach an audience of nearly 17 million but, later, attracted some criticism for allegedly demeaning black people.

Stratford Johns, Detective Chief Inspector Barlow, in the gritty police series, *Z Cars*

These programmes demonstrated the value of public service broadcasting where, unlike the unregulated American commercial system, patient experiment was possible and encouraged. It took time to build big audiences but BBC managers pointed out that such programme ideas would not have survived a single month in a fiercely competitive system. Some American series were, however, popular in Britain. *Dr Kildare*, a hospital soap opera, ran from 1961 to 1966, gaining a large following and showing that the British public wanted the best entertainment from any country.

An altogether different and stoutly British 'doctor' series was *Dr Who,* a science-fiction series which developed a cult following and drew loud protests when discontinued. Police series had begun with *Dixon of Dock Green* in the mid-Fifties but, in the Sixties, the more naturalistic and gritty approach seen in *Z Cars* and its spin-off series *Softly Softly* produced large audiences and some vociferous complaints. The police became one of the first professional groups in society to suffer what some saw as the indignity of 'faction' treatment.

The first *Dr Who*, William Hartnell, and his companions encounter the Daleks in an episode from 1963

Contemporary drama which caused a stir: *Cathy Come Home*, with Ray Brooks and Carol White

The Wednesday Play, a long-running series of single plays on BBC1, under the guidance of Sydney Newman, who was brought over from ITV, concentrated on contemporary themes and caused a particular stir in 1965 and 1966 with *Up the Junction* and *Cathy Come Home*. These, and many other productions in the series, focused on 'the working man and woman' as 'a fit subject for drama', offending many because of the rawness of much of the language and behaviour.

Dixon of Dock Green (Jack Warner): Highly popular in the Fifties, the series faded as more naturalistic police series came along

Pete Murray: One of Radio 1's first DJs

Drama also flourished on radio in the 1960s, with numerous young playwrights such as Harold Pinter and Tom Stoppard being given their first commissions. *The Dales* replaced *Mrs Dale's Diary* as a big audience-puller. New kinds of broadcast journalism were heard in *The World at One*, which began in 1965, with *The World This Weekend* following in 1967. Change, however, was not always easy and in 1964 *Children's Hour* and the Features Department came to an end. The audience for the former was rapidly migrating to television programmes like *Blue Peter*, while the styles used by radio features were becoming more common throughout the service.

A rack used for storing records in the studio

Greene himself had introduced two important changes in radio. Both, for those who did not understand him, were apparently out of character. In 1959, as Director of News and Current Affairs, his job before he became Director-General, he had dropped the nine o'clock news in the Home Service, replacing it with a bulletin at 10, followed by a discussion. This was in response to a declining evening audience moving over to television and it led to accusations of betrayal. In the mid-Sixties Greene also claimed to have made a contribution to religious broadcasting by supporting the introduction of a popular hymn-singing programme, later called *Songs of Praise.* This, he claimed, arose from a conversation he had with Megan Lloyd George. As he wrote: 'I have been, and am, on the side of tolerance'.

Play School: A programme for young children transmitted on the second night of BBC2, 1964

In the last years of Greene's Director-Generalship there were important structural changes in radio which were to presage even more radical ones in the Seventies. In September 1967, Radio 1 began broadcasting, mainly as an answer to the flourishing pirate pop stations which had been outlawed by the Government in August that year. Radio 1 quickly attracted large audiences and new DJs, many of whom, like Tony Blackburn, had worked in pirate radio or for Radio Luxembourg. The former Light, Third and Home networks were retitled Radios 2, 3, and 4, but they continued to incorporate essential parts of their traditional output. Within three years they had developed into more obviously 'generic' stations, with distinct styles and contents that could be identified by their listeners. Radio 2 offered light entertainment, sport and news with a mixture of light music including jazz and swing; Radio 3 provided classical music, drama, talks and poetry; Radio 4 was the main vehicle for news, current affairs, documentaries, drama, comedy and talk shows. The Reithian pattern of a mixed mode of broadcasting was slowly being modified, with Radio 4, perhaps, remaining closest to that concept. Local radio started experimentally in 1967 at Leicester, mainly due to the energy and enthusiasm of Frank Gillard, the Managing Director of Radio.

The last two years of the Greene era were marked by other positive achievements, such as the introduction of colour to BBC2 in 1967 under the guidance of David Attenborough. A supplementary £5 licence fee for colour television was introduced, which enabled the BBC to look forward to an increased income.

After Lord Normanbrook died in June 1967, Lord Hill, a former Tory Minister, was appointed Chairman. In what was seen as a dramatic snub to Greene, Harold Wilson had moved Hill over from the Chairmanship of the 'opposition', the Independent Television Authority. Senior BBC staff compared the move to transferring Rommel to command the Eighth Army. Wilson denied ill-will, but it was known that he had been upset by the treatment dealt out to Labour politicians in satirical programmes such as *TW3* and in other broadcasts, especially in the 1966 General Election campaign. He was, however, to have much more to complain about in 1971 with the programme which caused one of the biggest political rows, *Yesterday's Men*.

Greene, knighted in 1964, was inclined to resign after the appointment of Hill but his colleagues persuaded him against it. He did not, however, achieve rapport with his new Chairman and left in early 1969, having become the first ex-Director-General to be appointed a Governor of the BBC. This was not a happy move and after becoming fairly critical of his old employer, Sir Hugh Greene severed official connection with the Corporation in 1971. Meanwhile Lord Hill was developing into a doughty defender of his new charge while introducing it to some new and unfamiliar management ideas which were revealed in the Broadcasting in the Seventies debate.

Cliff Michelmore surveys Studio 1, BBC Television Centre: The hub of the 1966 Election Results Service

An early Philips colour camera

Dr Charles Hill MP broadcasting in 1950. He was the Radio Doctor during the war and later became BBC Chairman

A Murphy television set which came in coloured cabinets

Technological Triumphs

Visitors often remark on the high quality of British radio sound and television pictures; this is mainly due to the work of the engineers and the engineering practices used in the broadcasting industry. The BBC's first Director-General was an engineer, and great emphasis has always been placed on the technical quality of the BBC's work, which is the essential base on which all productions rest. Without studios, transmitters, microphones, cameras, recorders and all the hardware, there would simply be nothing for the public to hear and see.

BBC engineers are not, and cannot be, back-room boffins, although there has been an Engineering Research Department in the Corporation since the earliest days. The key tasks are to ensure that the BBC has the best equipment available and to keep it operating to the highest possible standards. This is done in close co-operation with the British radio and television industry and much benefit has also come from the work done by broadcasting engineers in Europe, the USA and Japan. All this was vividly demonstrated in the Sixties when some outstanding technical developments took place, including the gradual introduction of Very High Frequency (VHF) transmissions, of colour television and of stereo sound. These, and other examples obvious to the listener and viewer, were the result of much research and experiment and were linked with less visible but equally significant developments, many of them very complex and invisible to the general public. Much of this work received recognition in the industry, winning awards comparable to those won for radio and television programmes.

BBC engineers, often in collaboration with others including those in the independent sector, have been awarded Queen's Awards to Industry; one came in 1969 for a device called field-store standards converter, used in 1968 for the transmission by satellite of transatlantic colour television pictures from the Mexico Olympic Games. This enabled the exchange of programmes, both live and recorded, between different countries which, through the various accidents of history, had developed different systems of constructing television pictures. Some, for example, broke the screen image into 405 lines, some 525, and

The first 'consumer' video-recorder, from Philips

Splicing block for editing 2-inch videotape before electronic editing was introduced

Robin Day introduces an edition of *Panorama* in 1967

others 625. Without a conversion device, interchanging pictures between countries and systems would be impossible and the richness of modern television would have been much reduced.

Another technical innovation which had a profound effect on all aspects of radio and television production was video-recording using magnetic tape. In the Sixties, significant advances were made in this electronic recording of pictures, just as between the Forties and Fifties the recording of sound on tape was immeasurably improved. Although the system of picture recording developed by BBC research engineers was eventually overtaken by an American system, it played an important role in the process of ensuring that the BBC had the best technology available. Sound recording had become essential in the Empire Service because of the problem of transmitting programmes over large areas split into different time zones. Other advantages soon became clear, such as the possibility of editing programmes by cutting tape, compiling programmes from different sources and storing programmes for repeat and archival purposes. All these options became essential in television as well as in sound radio and, from 1947 onwards, following American practice, film recording was commonly used at the BBC. Telerecording, as it was known, was a clumsy device, although some early television programmes, fortunately, were preserved in this way. It became clear that American engineers in the late Forties were working on a totally electronic system, using magnetic tape instead of film, similar to the system used in sound recording.

BBC engineers began working on their magnetic tape recorder, called VERA (Vision Electronic Recording Apparatus), in 1952 and by 1958 were able to demonstrate it to the press. It was used shortly afterwards in a *Panorama* programme, but the image of Richard Dimbleby projected on the screen (a 'repeat' of his live performance a few minutes previously), was thought to be fuzzy and no better than the best film telerecording. Events overtook the team working on this project when the Ampex Corporation in America made public

Raymond Baxter, pictured beside models of Telstar and Mariner II, introduces the *Challenge* programme in 1963

their superior system. BBC engineers saw its power, placed orders, and by October 1958 the first machine was being used successfully at the Lime Grove studios. Television production was transformed in the next few years and live programmes, apart from news and current affairs, became rarer. As with all electronic devices, reductions in size gradually became possible. In 1974, BBC Engineering won its second Queen's Award to Industry for a new system of sound for television, called 'Sound-in-Sync', which allowed the sound signal to be carried as an integral part of the visual signal. This not only produced better sound but reduced expenditure by cutting out the need for separate sound circuits – in turn simplifying programme distribution arrangements.

Among other important engineering projects carried out in the period 1955-1968 were:

Seen live via Telstar in 1962: The New York skyline

• Trials to select which of the colour television systems should be used in the UK.
• A better use of frequency-modulation (FM) and much higher frequency bands (VHF). These gave enhanced sound quality, especially desirable in radio music programmes, and helped to overcome problems associated with the 'cluttering' of the long and medium wavebands.
• Increasing research and development in the use of satellites in broadcasting, begun in 1962 with Telstar, an American satellite, which had been used to transmit television pictures across the Atlantic to Europe. Satellite broadcasting was to open new windows on a world increasingly covered by global communications.
• Investigation into the use of transistors, invented in America in 1948, which were to transform receivers of all kinds and make portable and car radios commonplace.
• Early work on the teletext system Ceefax, which uses the domestic television screen to provide the public with up-to-date textual information and which began in 1972. Teletext developed slowly but surely over the next 20 years and is now available throughout the UK. Like several other new developments, it depended on the increased use of digitalisation, a new way of dealing with electrical information.

Index page of the 30-page experimental Ceefax service

7

new models

1968-1982

Broadcasting in the Seventies

This was the name given to a slim, innocuous-looking pamphlet published by the BBC in July 1969, which sought to explain a shift in policy, mostly relating to radio and regional broadcasting. It had been written by Ian Trethowan, a journalist, formerly of ITN, who had been selected to succeed Frank Gillard and who in 1977 would become Director-General. The new policy had derived from the work of a Policy Study Group, chaired by Gerard Mansell, then Controller Radio 4, which had as its members senior BBC executives, together with management consultants from the private company McKinsey. Lord Hill, the new Chairman, had proposed bringing in this company to study the BBC's financial and management arrangements.

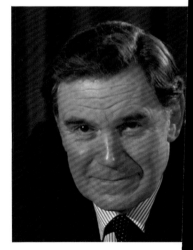

Ian Trethowan, Director-General, 1977-82

Many of the features of this development were, in fact, very unusual at the time. Taken separately and singly, they appeared relatively harmless; taken together they were more contentious and this may account for some of the arguments, inside and outside the BBC, that followed the publication of 'Broadcasting in the Seventies'. The proposed new policies were not universally welcomed, but it was the combination of new policies arrived at by new methods which led to what Lord Briggs, the historian of the BBC, has described as 'one of the most difficult controversies in its history'.

The new Director-General, Charles Curran, remarked soon after his appointment in April 1969 that this was the first time an inquiry of this kind had been carried out by the BBC rather than by the Government. It had, however, arisen as a result of discussions between the Chairman and the Postmaster-General, following concerns about the effects of rising inflation and, for the BBC, unusually forceful policies being adopted by the staff unions. The former Staff Association, renamed the Association of Broadcasting Staff after the start of ITV, had affiliated to the TUC in 1963 and was fighting for membership against more militant unions. In 1967, at a time of severe wage restraint and deflation – as well as half-a-million unemployed – ABS members began for the first time to work to rule. In September 1969, negotiations for a pay increase broke down and the ABS called for the first-ever strike against the BBC.

Charles Curran, Director-General, 1969-77

Just as unusual was the action by Lord Hill, a former Conservative politician, in putting his proposals for financial investigation to the vote at a Board of Governors' meeting. New, too, was the linking of BBC management with outside consultants in a study group, which was followed by a summary written by a new senior member of staff, Trethowan, who, like Hill, had been associated with 'the opposition'. Greene did not cross swords with his Chairman on this issue, recognising the seriousness of the position facing the BBC, an organisation whose problems, in the view of Charles Curran, did not arise from its size (it had over 23,700 staff when he was appointed) but, rather, from its complexity.

As Curran indicated later when he called his book on the BBC *A Seamless Robe*, no single strand of the Director-General's job could be entirely separated from other strands. For this and other reasons, he vigorously resisted the appointment of a deputy, which Charles Hill favoured.

Between 1968 and 1970, McKinsey prepared more than one report on the BBC in the course of thorough, friendly but costly investigations. Their first report in February 1970 is particularly interesting in view of subsequent events. Because of the large amount of creative talent involved in making programmes, McKinsey concluded that it was impossible to establish the optimum cost of the product, especially as, unlike most other organisations, the BBC had no direct link between its revenue and expenditure. Moreover, there was always uncertainty about future levels of income as Governments were reluctant to make licence increases. McKinsey pointed out the uniqueness of the Corporation, a non-profit making public body which had to spend the licence-payers' money efficiently.

McKinsey concluded that the BBC did this, and that it was probably the best broadcasting organisation in the world. 'You can't expect anything much more than that', observed Greene. While giving their clients an almost clean bill of health, the consultants had made suggestions for improvements in their earlier diagnostic studies. Authority should be more devolved, the organisational structure realigned, information systems for managers improved and continuous monitoring introduced to ensure economies.

The Radio 1 'family', on the station's 10th birthday

Among Radio 2's favourite voices: John Dunn (above) and Jimmy Young (below)

The key recommendation, eventually approved by the Government, was that those Directors who ran the three great output departments, Radio, Television and External Services, should be given more devolved power, be called Managing Directors and have control of their own budgets and engineering operations. This meant a shift of power away from the centrally placed Director-General, and this was not easy for Charles Curran to deal with. Less flamboyant than Hugh Greene, he already had to work with a Chairman who was taking a more interventionist role than his predecessor.

On policy matters two areas were selected as needing further investigation, and it was these which mainly preoccupied the Policy Study Group when it began work in November 1968: the future of radio, including the cost of music, and the role of the regions. Within four months the Group came back with costed recommendations for change, also covering a fundamental issue which had been identified by McKinsey: the possibility of funding the BBC by revenue from advertising. Curran wholeheartedly rejected the idea, writing in the BBC Handbook for 1970: 'Commercial financing for the BBC would be a form of slow suicide'.

'The Campaign for Better Broadcasting' was set up in the second half of 1969 to resist the changes being proposed under 'Broadcasting in the Seventies'. The signatories of a letter sent to *The Times* in September included Sir Adrian Boult, George Melly, Dr Jonathan Miller and Henry Moore – their concerns being cultural ones. Financial control, management restrictions and the devolution of power, subjects which had preoccupied McKinsey, the Policy Study Group and other parallel studies were of far less interest. The 'unique role' of the BBC would be threatened if, as had been suggested in 'Broadcasting in the Seventies', Radios 1, 2, 3 and 4 were made more 'generic'; if, instead of supporting 12 orchestras, the BBC in future supported only five, the shortfall in music airtime being made up by increased 'needletime' (ie the use of recordings); and if the three existing English Regions were to be replaced by eight smaller ones. The arguments became passionate, especially as jobs, particularly musical jobs, were involved. After protracted negotiations involving the Musicians' Union, modest changes were made in the music policy and the

BBC Symphony Orchestra (rehearsing here with conductor Pierre Boulez) is the flagship of the BBC's orchestras

Radio 3 announcer Patricia Hughes

Film-star Sophia Loren joins Richard Baker on *Start the Week*

Postmaster-General Edward Short attends the opening of Radio Leicester, the BBC's first local radio station, on 8 November 1967

proposed organisation of the English Regions went ahead. The eight new smaller regions concentrated on local television news and local 'opt-out' programmes as alternatives to the networks. Regional radio was gradually replaced by local radio. The former regional HQs at Birmingham, Manchester and Bristol became Network Production Centres supplying radio and television programmes to the networks.

Meanwhile, the Chairman and Director-General, concerned by the BBC's finances which had moved into the red, in August 1969 negotiated an increase in the licence fee. In 1969, the combined radio and colour television fee rose from £10 to £11, and in 1971 from £11 to £12. This helped to pay for the second phase of the BBC's plans to develop its local radio stations. In return, the BBC agreed not to proceed with most of its musical cuts, about which the Labour Government had been anxious, given the importance it attached to the views of the Musicians' Union.

The first experimental phase of the local radio plan meant building eight stations and there had been heated disputes about their funding – at one point local authorities were considered a suitable source. By November 1973, there were 20 stations; in 1978 the Callaghan Government authorised a further expansion. But, before this, in a 1971 White Paper, the Conservative Heath administration had proposed a larger network of commercial local radio stations, following this up in June 1972 with the Sound Broadcasting Act. This established Independent Local Radio (ILR), to be supervised by the Independent Television Authority (ITA), renamed the Independent Broadcasting Authority (IBA).

The early Seventies were important years for broadcasting. In 1971, the radio-only licence was abolished on grounds of economy; in 1972 the Post Office control of broadcasting hours ended; in 1974 departmental responsibility for broadcasting passed from the Ministry of Posts and Telecommunications, which was wound up, to the Home Office, thereby enhancing the importance of radio and television development within the Government hierarchy. Broadcasting was now set in a mould which would last many years.

Glenda Jackson had to spend hours in make-up for her transformation into *Elizabeth R*

The death of Lord Reith in 1971 marked, at least symbolically, the breaking of an earlier mould. It was a year in which some programme events, such as the screening of the magnificent *Elizabeth R* series and the start of Open University programmes on radio and television would have pleased him. Others, like the showing of *Yesterday's Men,* which provoked a furious row with the Labour Party, would have angered him. The setting up of the BBC Programmes Complaints Commission in October was a development about which he would have had mixed views.

The Virtue of Initiative

This was a phrase used by Charles Curran, writing in the 1970 BBC Handbook on 'A Decade in Prospect'. It headed a section dealing with 'the question of adventurousness in programmes' and 'the taking of calculated risks in the interest of liveliness and relevance'. The words of a former chairman of the Australian Broadcasting Commission were quoted: 'We do not regard our function as achieved if we merely keep out of trouble'. While arguing for the classic BBC virtue of balance, Curran denied that 'balance' implied 'fence-sitting' and urged producers to 'scorn the safety of dug-outs and prepared positions, if they have it in them to be genuinely creative'.

These remarks are an apt introduction to a period in which there was much innovation and initiative, accompanied by increasing criticism of television. Unease about some programmes grew into major controversy but, at a calmer level of debate, a greater number of articles and serious books were written about broadcasting and its social effects. The questions of how to deal with complaints and how control should be exercised began to be debated. But the main story in this period is one of successful and vigorous new programming, accompanied by the broadcasting of regular old favourites. Between 1968/9 and 1981/2, the hours of BBC annual transmission by the two home output departments increased as follows:

	1968-1969	**1981-1982**
RADIO	22,833	134,653
TELEVISION	6,486	12,741

The External Services suffered cuts in 1981, reducing the number of foreign language services from 40 to 37, but the total number of annual broadcasting hours remained at about 37,000.

Audience numbers rose to record levels, as did the average number of hours spent listening and viewing. It was not uncommon for a 1970s television audience to reach 20 million and popular radio shows could still attract 5 million listeners. The amount of viewing time in hours per week for BBC television had increased from 7.4 in 1969 to 10 in 1982, while the comparable figures for radio were 8.5 and 7.7 – the reduction caused largely by the arrival of ILR in 1973. Audiences for External Services programmes, often transmitting to countries with repressive regimes where listening to the BBC was difficult, were less easily measured, but in 1982 the BBC's world audience, tuning in regularly at least once a week, was estimated at around 100 million.

It is possible to pick out only a few examples of notable programmes in what became by the Eighties a vast and varied output. These years were particularly difficult ones for the country, with the oil crisis of 1973, for example, followed by a critical economic situation, a state of emergency and several strikes, a change from Conservative to Labour Government, and escalating violence in Northern Ireland. There was plenty for the news and current affairs departments to cover, but it was to light entertainment that the public overwhelmingly turned, presumably for relief.

An unusual Seventies television set

Harry H. Corbett and Wilfrid Brambell made *Steptoe and Son* the country's most famous rag-and-bone men

Open All Hours with David Jason and Ronnie Barker

Bill Oddie, Tim Brooke-Taylor and Graeme Garden brought surreal humour to BBC2 with *The Goodies*

The Two Ronnies (Corbett and Barker) was one of the most successful light entertainment shows of the period

Morecambe and Wise: Eric and Ernie in their own show

It Ain't Half Hot Mum dared to make fun of racial stereotypes

Fawlty Towers with Prunella Scales, John Cleese, Connie Booth and Andrew Sachs

The largest BBC television audience during Christmas 1973 was recorded on Christmas Day for the Queen's Broadcast followed by *The Morecambe and Wise Show*. This was 25 million, a huge but not entirely surprising figure given the traditional popularity of the BBC at this time of the year. *The Mike Yarwood Show* and *Miss World* achieved comparable figures, but the latter, although it remained popular for many years and achieved audience figures well over 20 million, fell victim to charges of sexism in the Eighties, a significant indication of changing attitudes.

Other successful light entertainment series of the period were *Up Pompeii!* with Frankie Howerd in an unlikely Roman format, *The Two Ronnies*, *Bruce Forsyth and the Generation Game*, *It Ain't Half Hot Mum,* which dared to make fun of racial stereotyping and *Hi-de-Hi!,* which set its traditional broad humour in a holiday camp. Breaking new ground in innovative comedy were *Monty Python's Flying Circus*, *The Goodies*, *Fawlty Towers* and *Not the Nine O'Clock News*. Contrasting situation comedies also flourished at this time, as shown by the success of *The Liver Birds*, *The Last of the Summer Wine*, *The Good Life*, *Open All Hours*, *The Fall and*

The Generation Game, with Bruce Forsyth and Anthea Redfern

Bill Oddie, John Cleese, Tim Brooke-Taylor, Jo Kendall, Graeme Garden and producer David Hatch rehearse Radio 2's *I'm Sorry I'll Read that Again*

Barry Took chairs Radio 4's *The News Quiz*

Comedy series *The Liver Birds* with Nerys Hughes and Polly James

The Fall and Rise of Reginald Perrin brought a tour-de-force performance from Leonard Rossiter

John Cleese's 'silly walk': Perhaps the single best-remembered moment from the anarchic *Monty Python's Flying Circus*

The Good Life, starring Felicity Kendal, Richard Briers, Penelope Keith and Paul Eddington

Rise of Reginald Perrin, *Butterflies*, *Yes Minister* and *Only Fools and Horses*. Most of these series made stars of the leading performers, had their formats and style copied and have been repeated over the years to great acclaim. It delights critics to accuse the BBC and ITV of using repeats improperly but they often achieve larger audiences than the original transmission.

Radio experimented with new forms of comedy and introduced not only disc-jockeys like Kenny Everett (who got into trouble in 1970 for making a joke on Radio 1 about a politician's wife) but also long-running series such as *I'm Sorry I Haven't a Clue, I'm Sorry I'll Read that Again, The News Quiz* and *Quote – Unquote*. 1972 also witnessed *The Last Goon Show of All* and Radio 2 became the first all-night broadcasting network in Britain in 1978.

Drama, too, had many successes in terms both of audience figures and critical recognition. In 1969, Shaun Sutton, the Head of Television Drama Group, described BBC television drama as 'The Theatre in the Living Room' and later as 'The Largest Theatre in the World'. It was a major achievement

Keith Michell as Henry VIII (with Annette Crosbie, Dorothy Tutin and Anne Stallybrass as three of his wives) made *The Six Wives of Henry VIII* an international best-seller

Dennis Potter's *Pennies from Heaven* (with Bob Hoskins and Cheryl Campbell) broke new ground in drama

Grange Hill: Delighting most children, if not always figures of authority, since 1978

Softly Softly was the successor to *Z Cars* in realistic police drama

On the set of BBC1's drama series *Colditz*

to attract audiences of between 2.7 and 6.4 million to series such as *The Six Wives of Henry VIII* and *Elizabeth R.* No doubt these colourful productions, which have been repeated frequently and sold around the world, appealed through their evocation of a glorious, historical past. More people saw Shakespeare performed than ever before when all his 37 plays went into production from 1978 onwards. There were even more viewers for contemporary material: police series such as *Softly Softly* and early catastrophe serials such as *Doomwatch* achieved audiences of between 7 and 12 million in 1970. Contemporary playwrights like

Dennis Potter and Ian Curteis, writing from quite different political standpoints, had major successes with *Pennies from Heaven* and *Suez 1956.* Other notably popular drama series and serials of the decade were *The Brothers, When the Boat Comes In, The Onedin Line, Colditz, The Pallisers* (representing another attractive genre, the dramatisation of classic novels), *Glittering Prizes, Testament of Youth* and *Tinker, Tailor, Soldier, Spy.* Two of Tolstoy's masterpieces, *War and Peace* and *Anna Karenina,* were also dramatised, the first also being turned into a radio serial in 1969. In children's television, *Grange Hill* made its first appearance

The *Family*, Paul Watson's celebrated documentary series, was an early example of fly-on-the-wall techniques

The *Blue Peter Royal Safari* in 1971 covered Princess Anne's first solo foreign visit

BBC2's cult rock music show *The Old Grey Whistle Test*

Life on Earth: David Attenborough on location

Suez 1956: A television play by Ian Curteis

in 1978 and has continued ever since, raising many questions and a few worries for some parents and teachers, but delighting most children.

Another important genre which grew in stature during the Seventies was the filmed drama-documentary tracing a life or sequence of historical events, such as *The Search for the Nile, The Explorers* and *The Voyage of Charles Darwin.* In the purer documentary form there was *The Royal Family, Blue Peter Royal Safari, The Family* (an early example of the fly-on-the-wall technique in filming), *Sailor* (a study of naval life), and David Attenborough's *Life on Earth,* which was accompanied by a hugely successful book.

In music and the arts notable broadcasts included *André Previn's Music Night,* a production of Benjamin Britten's opera *Owen Wyngard,* and *The Young Musician of the Year* competition which still flourishes, while *The Old Grey Whistle Test* appealed to rock fans. *The Shock of the New,* presented by the critic Robert Hughes, described the development of modern art, and *Timewatch* explored various approaches to history.

Songs of Praise from St Mary's Church, Banbury

Phil Drabble (left) in *One Man and His Dog*

The famous *Mastermind* black chair

Alongside the long-running sports favourites, *Pot Black* and *One Man and His Dog* created big audiences for new indoor and outdoor interests, while *Mastermind* tested competitors in an original and popular format. *The Antiques Roadshow, That's Life!* and *Jim'll Fix It* were other more general offerings which remained popular television into the Nineties, together with *Kaleidoscope, Checkpoint, Start the Week,* and *Stop the Week* on radio.

This formidable output, which could not be equalled by any other broadcasting organisation, includes some of the more popular home-made entertainment programmes of the Seventies. However, current affairs and politics were strong and innovative, too, as were American bought-in programmes such as *M.A.S.H.* and *Kojak.* There were important additions to regular political programming, notably the replacement of *Tonight* by *Nationwide* in 1969. This very successful early-evening programme incorporated reports from all the

Esther Rantzen outside BBC Television Centre for *That's Life!*

Popular into the Nineties: Jimmy Savile's *Jim'll Fix It*

The Antiques Roadshow: A programme which has lost none of its popularity

Pot Black: Television boosted snooker

Monday-to-Friday current affairs magazine
Nationwide (with presenter Michael Barratt)
brought reports from the regions

Bob Hoskins in *On The Move*, the award-winning
television programme for people with reading difficulties

oes He Take Sugar?: A pioneering series
for people with disabilities

Reporters Mike Dornan and Eric Robson, with
presenter Brian Trueman got to the heart of the
headlines for *Brass Tacks*, live from Manchester

Open Door began in 1973, helping groups to
make their own television programmes

regions and showed them in a national context. Also from the regions came the hard-hitting *Brass Tacks,* produced by the Network Production Centre in Manchester, which had been opened in 1976 by the Prime Minister, James Callaghan. Series like *Analysis, International Assignment, File on 4* and *Feedback* all started on radio in the Seventies.

In the area of social concern, there were several new broadcasting initiatives which have lasted. On radio, *You and Yours* replaced the long-running series *Can I Help You?,* addressing a wide range of welfare, health and consumer issues, and *Does He Take Sugar?* became the first general series for people with disabilities. The Education Departments were also alert to the need to help those who required it and they mounted major projects for adults with reading difficulties, old people, trade-unionists and many other groups which were often ignored. For those who wanted to make a fresh start in more academic fields, the BBC joined with the new Open University to produce multi-media learning packages and the first radio and television transmissions began in 1971. Within years the Open University became a great success.

One other programme area, which was later to flourish, started in the Seventies. The climate of the time and the example of what was happening in the US and Europe nourished the idea that ordinary citizens should have a more significant role in programme-making and, as a result, 'access' broadcasting began on both BBC and ITV, together with programmes which questioned the professional programme-makers. At the BBC 'access' flourished from 1973 as *Open Door,* with the BBC's Community Programme Unit helping groups to make their own programmes, while phone-in and feedback programmes proliferated. These were all examples of the opening up or democratising of broadcasting, which was to feature prominently in future media debates.

Controversies and Research

In over a decade of expansion and innovation, it was inevitable that there would be criticism from some viewers. Listeners had fewer complaints, apart from a concern about a freer use of 'bad language', an area which was, and remains, the cause of most dissatisfaction about both radio and television output. The complaints and the controversies (always 'rows' in the tabloid press) that sometimes accompanied them began, increasingly, to be about the portrayal of violence and sex, political bias and the effects of excessive television viewing on family life.

Later, in the Eighties, sexism and racism gave cause for concern. Pressure groups were formed, often representing relatively small but vociferous clusters of people. Genuine research, another developing and valuable activity, almost invariably showed that the great majority of the public was more than happy with what the BBC and ITV were providing. But individual politicians of both major parties persuaded themselves that the BBC and ITV were biased to the right or to the left. Intellectuals and academics entered the debate, with those holding radical left-wing views tending to be more active in the Seventies, while those with vocal right-wing views counter-attacked in the Eighties.

Some criticisms were, of course, justified, but it became time-consuming to answer every single charge and the broadcasting authorities responded in a number of ways. In 1971, for example, the BBC set up an Advisory Group on the Social Effects of Television and its own Programmes Complaints Commission. Apart from the work of its increasingly important and influential Broadcasting Research Department (formerly Audience Research Department), the BBC combined with the IBA and others in 1981 to set up an independent Broadcasting Research Unit.

The first BBC code on the portrayal of violence was published as early as 1960, revised in 1972 on the advice of the Advisory Group on the Social Effects of Television, and again in 1979 and in the Eighties. Largely influenced by the next Government-sponsored Committee of Enquiry into broadcasting under Lord Annan, a completely new and, at the time, contentious approach to research began in 1981 with the Broadcasters' Audience Research Board, in which the two sides of the duopoly co-operated.

The Annan Committee Report, published in 1977, shows very clearly the change in attitudes which had taken place since the Pilkington Committee Report in 1962, placing as it did much more emphasis on criticism of the media and the importance of researching the facts. But research, although often very expensive, could not get at all the facts and answer all the questions. It became obvious that subjective value-judgements were inevitable in most matters of taste and morality and no amount of scientific measurement would provide definitive answers. For example, was it right for the BBC School Broadcasting Departments in 1969 to provide sex education programmes for eight-year-olds? Most teachers thought it was but the critics complained loudly. More importantly for the politicians, was it right for television producers to investigate their private lives or to make programmes which appeared to them to 'interfere with' Government policies? These last two issues led to the most controversial and, some said, damaging arguments between politicians and the BBC in the Seventies.

Yesterday's Men, a television documentary, was made after the defeat of the Labour Government under Harold Wilson in 1970 and transmitted on 17 June 1971. It provoked a furious debate in the press and in Parliament, involved many people in the BBC from the producer and presenter upwards to the Board of Governors, changed the career of at least one senior manager and led another to conclude that 'it did us great harm'. The chief purpose of the programme was to show how losing office affected the lives of Government Ministers. Harold Wilson and his ex-Cabinet colleagues including James Callaghan, a future Labour Prime Minister, Denis Healey and Barbara Castle took part and were filmed explaining how their incomes and lifestyles had been changed.

On the one hand it became clear that they did not find the transition to opposition life as painless as their Conservative counterparts, who, they felt, were generally offered comfortable alternative employment in the City and elsewhere. On the other hand their lifestyles appeared to be relatively affluent. Among several Labour objections were the satirical tone of the programme,

The *Radio Times* billing for *Yesterday's Men,* which brought the Labour Party into conflict with the BBC

with a song composed by 'The Scaffold' pop group, and the demeaning title. The participants felt deceived. The phrase 'Yesterday's Men' had, in fact, been used by the Labour Party in 1970, when it expected to win the General Election, to describe the Conservatives, so the irony was particularly painful. To make it worse, in the eyes of Labour, a programme of a gentler tone about Edward Heath and his Government was transmitted a day later. Harold Wilson had

been particularly upset by questioning from David Dimbleby, the presenter of the programme, on the money he had earned from writing a book about his term of office, and the BBC agreed to edit part of the filmed interview. There were threats of legal action, with damages demanded and refused, but an apology was made. This sorry story was further complicated by internal arguments about the involvement of the BBC Governors, some of whom saw the film before transmission, a most unusual occurrence.

The episode raised questions about the relationship between producers and politicians and between the Board of Governors and BBC executives. One important consequence was the demand for a Broadcasting Council to stand as judge in such matters. Early in 1971, the BBC Chairman, Lord Hill, had raised the question of an 'external scrutinising board', something like the Press Council, and various examples of how individuals who had claimed to be wronged in BBC broadcasts were studied. There can be little doubt that, as Lord Hill wrote in his broadcasting memoirs: 'Yesterday's Men had stimulated fresh demands for an appellate body'. The BBC Programmes Complaints Commission, consisting of three independent and distinquished public figures, was set up in October 1971 and lasted until 1981 when the Government-backed Broadcasting Complaints Commission began its work.

The Question of Ulster, a three-hour live television programme transmitted on 5 January 1972, raised different

112

and in many ways more fundamental issues. Here, policy and not personality was involved. The conflict was with Mr Heath's Conservative Government over an issue, the crisis in Northern Ireland, which has dominated political controversy in broadcasting matters to the present day. In this case the BBC Governors and senior executives were in agreement, and despite attempts by the Home Secretary, Reginald Maudling, to get the BBC to scrap the prog-

ramme, it went ahead. Most observers concluded this was certainly the right decision, despite some misgivings about the programme's length.

With the background of the extremely violent situation developing in Northern Ireland and the increased death-rate, there was much to be said for a long, cool, look at events, and that is what was planned. It was felt that the reporting of day-to-day violence and rioting could usefully be complemented by discussion, analysis and

The Question of Ulster (introduced by Ludovic Kennedy) looked at possible solutions to the problems in Northern Ireland

argument, with an emphasis on the future and possible solutions, rather than the past and recriminations. The format of the programme was conventional and non-controversial: after Ludovic Kennedy set the scene, three distinguished public men, a judge and two senior politicians, one from each of the two main parties, listened to statements from representatives from all the main Irish

political interests. Questions were allowed and a summing-up given at the end. But before the programme even got to the screen, the Government expressed disquiet because the word 'tribunal' was used to describe the format – a technical inaccuracy because no judgement was to be given. The description was dropped, but some damage had been done, with the programme being perceived as an infringement of Government responsibilities.

While attempts to persuade the BBC against making the programme continued, the producer had difficulty in getting representatives to give Westminster's and Stormont's cases. It seemed that the programme would have to be cancelled through non-co-operation, a technique which was to be much used in the future by politicians of all kinds who had objections to taking part in discussion programmes. However, within days of the promised transmission, the problem was solved to the satisfaction of both the BBC management and Governors. In the event, all the important points of view were heard and questioned, those of the extreme wings of the Unionist and Nationalist camps were evidently as far apart as ever, and no solution emerged. A decent and fairly well-mannered debate had taken place, the Government had over-reacted and, given the large audience of 7.5 million that had started watching the pro-gramme, the streets of Northern Ireland remained quieter than usual.

The problem of reporting and analysing the Northern Ireland crisis would not easily

Late Sixties: The first all-transistor colour television, from Thorn

disappear. At a dinner given by the BBC in Belfast in November 1976, the Labour Secretary of State for Northern Ireland, Roy Mason, surprised the BBC Governors and staff present by accusing them of disloyalty in the battle against terrorism. Reminding them of the coming need to renew the Charter and Licence and to increase the licence fee, he made it plain that the Government held the whip-hand. It was a threat which would be used again by other Ministers.

Apart from the clashes with politicians, fundamental questions about broadcasting were now being asked by a wide range of people. Media research had begun in earnest at British universities in the mid-Sixties, the Social Morality Council was set up in 1966 to monitor the effects of broadcasting and in the Seventies books on the subject poured from the publishers. Robin Day, a central figure in television, began to ask questions in 1975 about 'the lie of the image' and 'the craving for pace' while, in a series of influential articles in *The Times* in the same year, John Birt of London Weekend Television joined with Peter Jay, an economist, to question the 'bias against understanding' in much television current affairs. Both were, in the future, to hold prominent positions in the BBC.

The broadcasters were on the defensive and the situation underlined a charge made by Anthony Wedgwood Benn in 1968 when he was Minister of Technology: 'Broadcasting is really too important to be left to the broadcasters'. It was this kind of assertion, among many others, that the Committee under the chairmanship of Lord Annan now investigated. The BBC prepared its evidence with thoroughness, knowing this was not going to be a re-run of the Pilkington enquiry.

Annan and After

The Committee on the Future of Broadcasting under Lord Annan began its work in 1974 – a year as turbulent as any in the early Seventies. Indeed, turbulence, crisis and rapid development were all to become standard in the following two decades, mainly because of fundamental technological, economic and political changes.

The BBC had its own particular problems, described by Sir Michael Swann when, as a relatively new Chairman, he wrote of 1974: 'The last year has not been an easy one for Britain, and that inevitably means difficult times for the British Broadcasting Corporation. Because of inflation, and in spite of economies, our financial position has become increasingly gloomy; and in the present year it can be expected to reach crisis proportions, leading to massive cuts in programmes, unless the licence fee is raised'.

The Fifth Charter of 1964, granted for 12 years after the Pilkington enquiry, was soon due for renewal (in fact, it was extended twice, until 1981). Costs were rising fast, industrial action becoming more common and, by 1976, the BBC was driven to borrowing money for the first time. In October 1974 the BBC was strongly criticised by the Labour Government for awarding staff what it saw as an excessive pay increase and it issued a report after the General Election alleging anti-Labour bias in BBC coverage. Fortunately, the relationships between Sir Michael Swann and the Directors-General who worked under him, Charles Curran (knighted in 1974) and Ian Trethowan (knighted in 1980), were good, the management team was strong and the quality of programming as high as it had ever been.

Despite having less money than ITV, the BBC on its two television channels generally maintained a 50/50 share of the audience with ITV's one, while the new independent local radio stations had yet to make significant inroads into the BBC's radio audience. Nationally and internationally, the Corporation continued to win the majority of prizes and, despite cuts, the External Services remained high in world esteem. Annan and his colleagues at times even noted a certain self-satisfaction and arrogance in their meetings with the BBC.

The Annan Committee had an unusual history, having originally been set up by the Wilson Government in May 1970. Following its victory in the General Election of the following month, the new Heath Government stood the Committee down and it was not reconvened until July 1974 by the new Labour Government. Here was a prize example of the 'stop-go' politics which characterised the period. By the time the Annan Committee did get into its stride there had been a House of Commons Select Committee report demanding more accountability by the broadcasters, an official recommendation that the technical standards on television should be enhanced and support given for cable and satellite broadcasting. In 1974 another report recommended that a fourth television channel should be provided in Wales with programmes in the Welsh language, to be produced by both the BBC and ITV. The larger question of how a fourth television channel for the whole United Kingdom should be organised was a prime question for Annan.

Sir Michael Swann, BBC Chairman, Lord Annan and the IBA's Lady Plowden discuss the Annan Report in Radio 4's *Analysis*

In its submissions to the Committee, the BBC, as the Report explained, 'disclaimed any wish to have the responsibility for a fourth channel' and proposed a form of super educational channel. Along with others, it argued against a second ITV. But much had changed in the years between 1973, when the original Committee might have reported, and 1977 when in fact it did report. Cultural and social issues were becoming less important than economic and technical ones, a change in mood reflected by the fact that, unlike previous wide-ranging reports on broadcasting, this one was peppered with Notes of Dissent and even a Note of Reservation on the actual recommendations from one member.

The Committee, which included MPs and political figures of different persuasions, academics, businessmen and several people with experience in radio and television, was not to be browbeaten. The spirit of the age of dissent was visible.

The work of the Committee was more comprehensive than that of earlier ones, and the Report contained 174 recommendations, compared with Beveridge's 100 and Pilkington's 120. It met 44 times in full session and 28 times in specialised groups, reviewing papers containing evidence and views from over 750 individuals and organisations. The chapter headings of the 522-page Report covered a very wide spectrum, including studies of particular types of programme, technical matters, industrial relations, audience research and programme journals. Although its two main recommendations – for a new Local Broadcasting

Authority to take over all the existing services from both the BBC and IBA, and for an Open Broadcasting Authority to operate a fourth television channel – were not taken up by the Government, it had a major influence on the future of broadcasting by opening up discussion on a broad range of topics which were to become important.

The BBC welcomed the Report's main findings and in particular the support given to the principles and programmes associated with the BBC, while noting various criticisms concerning 'loss of nerve' and 'organisational fog', which were said to have 'struck home'. Public service broadcasting, the licence fee and editorial independence from Government were all reaffirmed. Less welcome were the proposals regarding the need for a three-tiered system of broadcasting at national, regional and local levels, each with its own Authority. The Governors believed that, although the BBC was the premier national broadcaster, it had to have both regional and local roots: 'For us a "national" role cannot be purely metropolitan'.

The BBC also opposed proposals for improving its accountability to the public by the setting up of a Public Enquiry Board, which would have held regular public hearings on broadcasting issues, but it supported a new statutory and independent Broadcasting Complaints Commission. This was rather like the BBC's own complaints body and began operating in June 1981. An important Annan Committee proposal that was implemented was concerned with improving audience research. Its 170th recommendation asked that the two members of the duopoly 'at once devise a combined system for assessing audience ratings for all broadcast channels, and the consequent savings reallocated to other forms of audience research'. The Committee

had been vexed by the arguments generated by the two different methods of measurement then being used, acerbically noting that 'Commentators observe with some irony that the methods on which each system is based consistently produce the most favourable result for those who pay for it'. In July 1981 the Broadcasters' Audience Research Board (BARB), a joint BBC/ITV system, was established after much argument and negotiation, but whether it saved money or not is hard to judge.

Many members of Annan's Committee were also worried by the existence of two programme journals, *Radio Times* and *TV Times*. Their preferred solution was that the broadcasters should waive their copyright so that these publications could publish full listings of all radio and television programmes. The broadcasters resented the potential loss of income which would follow and the argument rumbled on into the Nineties.

The most important result of all the work done by Annan and his colleagues was the creation of Channel 4. It was not the outcome they proposed, but it was ingenious and benefited from the thoughts set down in the Committee Report. The IBA was authorised by the Broadcasting Act of 1980, passed during the early years of the new Conservative Government led by Margaret Thatcher, to establish the fourth channel, designed to be innovative and to complement ITV. Most of the programmes were to be made by new, smaller, independent companies, many pioneers having set out on this precarious path in the early Sixties. They were to become an increasingly important and powerful force in broadcasting.

Channel 4 was launched on 2 November 1982 and served

the whole of the United Kingdom except for Wales which, after intense political lobbying, had its own channel S4C (Sianel Pedwar Cymru) operated by its own Authority. The British broadcasting duopoly system now had a neat symmetry, with BBC1 matched by ITV and BBC2 matched by Channel 4. A new kind of ratings battle was about to be joined.

The years between the publication of the Annan Report (1977) and the beginning of the next phase in broadcasting, heralded by the start of Channel 4 and the emergence of significant new technical challenges, were marked by a series of financial and programme-related events which can be seen in retrospect both to typify the period and to provide pointers to the future.

In July 1978, less than a year before it lost power, the Labour Government issued a White Paper which acknowledged the BBC as 'arguably the single most important cultural organisation in the nation' and supported much of what Annan had proposed. This, along with the Government's commitment to a new Royal Charter in 1979, was good news for the BBC, but there was concern at the continuing uncertainty about the licence fee and a proposal for what were called Service Management Boards. These would have interposed a layer of Government-controlled supervision at high levels within the BBC output departments. The proposal vividly illustrates the desire politicians of all persuasions have to supervise the broadcast media.

As if to emphasise this, a sharp attack on the BBC came from the new Prime Minister, Mrs Thatcher, within months of her election victory in May 1979. On 30 March 1979, her close colleague, Airey Neave, had been murdered by a bomb planted by a small Irish terrorist group, the Irish National Liberation Army (INLA). A filmed interview with a hooded INLA spokesman, broadcast a few weeks later on the *Tonight* programme, had caused Mrs Thatcher and Lady Neave deep offence and the Director-General, Ian Trethowan, later agreed that he was wrong to have agreed to the transmission. The question of whether or not the undoubted news interest in interviews with terrorists justified their broadcast was urgently placed on the agenda. Coming as it did with other Northern Ireland incidents in 1979, right at the beginning of a new Conservative administration, this episode did not augur well for the future.

Enterprise Culture

Under the chapter heading 'BBC Finances', Annan referred briefly to some additions to the Corporation's licence fee income which it had noted. In the year ending March 1976 these amounted to £7.3 million, the total received from the issue of television licences having been £212.9 million. This additional 'small income', representing about one-thirtieth of the BBC's total income, came from 'the profit of its publications and overseas sales and from repayments by the Open University for the programmes which the BBC provides'. There was no suggestion in the recommendations that this source of income might usefully be increased.

The BBC had been making profits from sales of its publications since 1923 when *Radio Times* started and when publications began to be issued to supplement educational programmes for schools and adults. The first BBC Annual Report, published in 1928, when income from licences was about £801,000 and the circulation of *Radio Times* was

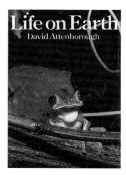

well over one million, records 'Net Revenue from Publications' as £93,686.l0.ld, about 10% of total income. From its inception in 1932, the Empire Service had published important periodicals such as *World Radio* and, later, *London Calling,* but because of its separate finances, money from the sale of these had no bearing on the BBC's home income.

By the Seventies, the output of Publications Department had become very large, with *Radio Times* the best-selling magazine in the country and a large number of educational and general publications proving highly profitable. Following the success of Sir Kenneth Clark's colour television series and book, *Civilisation,* in 1969, the number of bestsellers, particularly those related to television series on subjects such as cookery, gardening and language learning, had increased dramatically. Between 1972 and 1984, the number of books published annually doubled to 100. Nevertheless, BBC Publications, along with other publishers, suffered both from competition and from the worsening economic climate. *Radio Times* had an average weekly sale of 9 million in the mid-Fifties, but by the early Eighties this had dropped to 3.5 million. The arrival of *TV Times* with the start of ITV and the publication of daily schedules in newspapers had taken their toll.

In the early Seventies, income from Publications was over £1.5 million, but by 1974, amid industrial disruption, steeply rising prices and paper shortages, an unprecedented loss of £14,000 was sustained. Recovery came in the early Eighties with trading profits from Publications running at £4.7 million in 1982. In the late Eighties, as licence revenue failed to meet costs, it became increasingly important to find income to supplement the licence fee.

There was a second source of extra revenue to augment that made from publications, namely the income derived from the sale of radio and television programmes, generally in the form of exports abroad. At first, many complex problems hindered this activity, including union and copyright restrictions. By the Sixties, the technical situation had improved and in 1958 a Business Manager (Television Programmes) had been appointed. His job was to 'stimulate production of television programmes on film in Britain and the Commonwealth countries' and to be 'responsible for the negotiation and co-ordination of co-production projects'. This work involved buying and selling programmes and included liaison with the External Services, which were to develop important sales abroad of sound tapes, books and films teaching English to foreigners. Co-production and co-financing of television programmes in which, for certain transmission and other rights, non-BBC sources (usually American) put money into production, became an important way of paying for many expensive projects.

All this work began to develop more vigorously from 1960 onwards, the year when BBC Television Promotions was established with a General Manager. In the following year, the more appropriate name of BBC Enterprises was adopted. In its first year the new department sold 550 programmes overseas and followed this in 1961 with 1,200 sales to more than 50 countries. Many foreign viewers were now able to enjoy series such as *Face to Face* and *Hancock's Half-Hour.* By 1967, Television Enterprises claimed to be one of the world's biggest distributors of programmes, with the American public television and Australian markets successfully penetrated.

Radio was always going to be a smaller market, but at the end of 1965 Radio Enterprises was set up to cash in on the records boom of the Sixties. The BBC was receiving an increasing number of requests from record companies for permission to use either BBC signature tunes or programme extracts, and an area ready for exploitation was gradually marked out. When the first General Manager of Radio Enterprises retired in 1969, the small department was amalgamated with Television Enterprises and within three years the catalogue of records available for sale to the public increased from half a dozen to 130.

The BBC's major step into an increasingly market-oriented culture came in 1979, the year of Mrs Thatcher's victory, when BBC Enterprises became BBC Enterprises Ltd, a subsidiary company wholly owned by the BBC. By 1982, turnover had increased from £234,000 in 1960 to £23 million, and there were now nine sales divisions, including film, records and tapes, merchandising, home video, education and training, and exhibitions. Television sales accounted for 70% of the annual turnover. Offices were set up in Australia and Canada, with distributors in the USA, Japan and South America. Important co-operative ventures were also started with American pay cable companies. BBC Enterprises Ltd. had developed into an important supplementary source of finance for the BBC, particularly with its ability to feed back money into television production, now rapidly becoming an expensive and highly competitive international operation.

The 1983 BBC Handbook, reporting the details of the activities of BBC Enterprises in the previous year, had on its cover an artist's impression of the European Space

Agency's European Communication Satellite. Inside, a report from the BBC's New York office contained these words: 'America is awash with new companies and new corporate alliances attempting to exploit cable, direct broadcasting satellites and a host of other means of distribution. Some of them, at the same time, are attempting to defend their share of the market by applying new techniques to traditional broadcast services. By understanding the risks and pitfalls in America and translating this experience into the British context, we may learn to act more wisely as we face up to the national and international effects of rapid technological changes, which are political and social as well as economic. In the United States the rapid multiplication of the means of delivery has so far not been matched by a growth in good programming. As the audience is fragmented, those who are attempting to provide programmes to fill this greatly increasing capacity to deliver signals have trouble finding money to sustain quality programmes.'

As had happened so often, the USA was setting the pace in broadcasting technology, if not in programme quality, and Britain, along with the rest of the developed world, was having to follow. By the end of 1982 a number of important steps had been taken by the British Government which would profoundly affect all broadcasters and what audiences would see and hear for many years to come. In May 1981 HMSO published a Home Office study called 'Direct Broadcasting by Satellite', with a foreword by the Home Secretary, William Whitelaw, who was to be largely responsible for seeing through the Channel 4 arrangements.

For most British people, DBS, as it came to be called, was a completely new way of transmitting broadcast signals which, at first, had an aura of science fiction. It was to occupy much BBC time and attention, and the Sixth Royal Charter, granted in July 1981 after considerable negotiation and designed to last until 1996, allowed the Corporation to exploit the new technology. Shortly afterwards, the Chairman, George Howard, and Director-General, Ian Trethowan, were able to report that a new licence fee had been secured. This was to last for just over three years and followed several much shorter-term increases. It set the colour licence at £46 (up from £34) and the monochrome licence at £15 (up from £12). Apart from allowing for better long-term planning, and despite being, as usual, less than requested, the settlement, in the Chairman's words, 'did allow us to plan to maintain all our services, to restore some of the cuts previously made and to introduce some much-needed enhancements'.

In February 1982 the Information Technology Advisory Panel (ITAP) Report on Cable Systems was published by the Cabinet Office. The Prime Minister herself had announced the appointment of the Information Technology advisors in July 1981 and they, mostly businessmen, had worked rapidly. Their Report was speedily followed in October 1982 by another, the Inquiry into Cable Expansion and Broadcasting Policy, the so-called Hunt Report. The stage had been set for a fast-moving and, some thought, too hastily arranged drama. The BBC and IBA/ITV managers had much to think about.

8

market forces

1982-1992

New Technologies and Ideologies

In the last 13 years there has been a marked and relentless move away from previously held political, social and economic assumptions. One aspect of this change has been a shift in emphasis from the public to the private sector, with the result that public services, including public service broadcasting, have found themselves profoundly challenged.

Having originally, as a monopoly, disavowed competition, the BBC became a successful competitor in a duopoly. From 1979 onwards under a new Conservative administration, headed by a Prime Minister who rejected consensus and promoted choice through relatively unregulated competition and market forces, the Corporation had to learn to survive in a much tougher climate without damaging the basic principles on which it was founded.

The ideological change in political life was accompanied and reinforced by technical changes. With the passing of time, the international nature of these two interdependent changes became evident.

As is often the case, the new technologies were not so new in principle. Three particular developments had a profound affect on the BBC and also ITV: the video-cassette and video-recorder, cable, and satellite transmission. The use of computers in broadcasting also expanded rapidly. Video-recording had been around since the Fifties, but was now miniaturised and redeveloped for the home; cable transmission was older than wireless transmission; and satellites had been used in television from the early Sixties. By the Eighties, all were at a sufficiently advanced technical stage to be attractive economic propositions and they fitted neatly with the direction of current new political ideas. They offered more choice to viewers and listeners, and also long-term hopes of high profits. In addition, they promised an amalgamation of broadcasting and telecommunications, so heralding a new age of information technology. The television screen was promoted as a multi-purpose device which would bring entertainment, information, education, banking and shopping directly into the home.

All this made attractive political sense, except to those commentators who recalled the disappointments of previous technology revolutions. The problem for the 'old-fashioned' or conventional broadcasters was how the 'new' technologies would affect their operations, especially as they were by no means free agents. A strategy was needed which would show that public service broadcasting had an essential role in the new marketplace.

Storage and playback devices such as the video-cassette (and later the videodisc), together with the VCRs to play them, began to appear in the early Seventies offering a new independence to the British television viewer who now had four channels and would soon have many more from which to choose. By the early Eighties, over 5% of households had a VCR, a figure which had risen to 64% in the early Nineties. 'Self-scheduling' by the viewer, using off-air recorded cassettes, as well as purchased and rented videos, gained in popularity. The legal implications of all this were complex and largely ignored by the public; for professional broadcasters they were confusing and, in the long term, worrying. When viewing figures fell, even temporarily, as they did in the early Eighties, was it because of the programmes, the weather or because of the pattern of video use?

Satellite and cable distribution of radio and television signals, in contrast to that of terrestrial transmitters, offered a clearer threat to the BBC. In the case of video-cassettes, the broadcasters could do little more than defend their copyright and, later, sell their programmes in cassette form. Now they had to decide if and how they were to exploit the 'new' means of distribution which offered the viewers and listeners some advantages such as extra choice and some disadvantages such as extra expense.

The May 1981 Government publication 'Direct Broadcasting by Satellite' (DBS) had on its cover a drawing of a satellite very similar to the one shown on the front of the BBC's 1983 Handbook, and it was the DBS phenomenon which, of the three technological developments, most seriously involved the BBC. Since the days of Telstar in 1962, the Corporation's engineers and producers had built up a great deal of experience in the use of satellites. In May 1965 *Out of This World* was the first television transmission from the United States via the Early Bird geostationary satellite. Poised above the earth at 22,300 miles and rotating with the earth at the same speed instead of going around it, it was this type of satellite which was to be the crucial step

BBC
Annual Report and
Handbook 1983

Out of This World: Richard Dimbleby and the Television
Centre studio stand by for the inaugural Early Bird
satellite transmission from America

leading to DBS. By 25 June 1967 the BBC was able to mount *Our World*, the first worldwide television programme bringing together live pictures and messages from around the globe beamed up to and down from a 'mirror in the sky'.

The simple concept of the geostationary satellite had been proposed in 1945 by the science-fiction writer Arthur C. Clarke and, as a way of transmitting signals, it offered a number of advantages, notably that a very large area indeed, the 'footprint', could be covered by one transmission signal direct to homes equipped with a small dish-aerial; prior to DBS the signals received from satellites required large dishes. The May 1981 document described in detail what was now possible and set down five strategic options for moving ahead.

An international conference in Geneva in 1977 had drawn up a plan for DBS in which most countries of the world (excluding the Americas) were allocated specific satellite positions and frequencies. The five positions given to Britain would be able to provide five television channels as well as radio, and the BBC was entrusted with the development of two. This was deemed a modest strategy and had a start-up date of 1986.

Press briefing for *Our World*, the first live global hook-up, sponsored by the European Broadcasting Union, June 1967

Clearly all sorts of opportunities were opened up, including commercial ones for the aerospace and electronics industries; politically, with unemployment hovering around three million, this was important. But for the BBC, DBS meant new programme outlets for showing sport, new films, public events and carefully scheduled repeats. Much had to be planned, including finding rocket launchers to send up the satellite and, above all, the financial implications had to be closely studied. In accordance with its philosophy, the Government did not want to get involved financially, but insisted that a British satellite should be used. This alone caused immense difficulties, which led to the collapse of the initial scheme.

The technical standard to be used in DBS across the world had not been thought through, and a special Government Committee chaired by a retired civil servant, Sir Anthony Part, was speedily set up to find a solution. BBC engineers were involved. Simultaneously the Government was pressing ahead with plans for the development of the cable

industry as part of the information technology-led industrial revolution. In April 1983 a White Paper was issued on the cable question and in July 1984 the Cable and Broadcasting Act was passed. A Cable Authority was to be set up operating under a 'light touch' (that is, with few controlling regulations) and licences issued for a number of cable systems. Although cable development began slowly without the likelihood of substantial profits, there were increasing worries in Parliament and among broadcasters that events were developing too quickly and in an uncontrolled way. The new BBC Chairman, Stuart Young, in September 1984 spoke of 'a reluctant revolution' and the Director-General, Alasdair Milne, warned of the possibility of several cable and satellite channels all offering repeats of soap operas, the 'wall-to-wall Dallas' fear. The increasingly large number of so-called 'video nasties' appearing on the market at this time did not help to allay fears of the dangers. Cable and satellite became increasingly interlinked since, DBS apart, satellite signals from more powerful transmitters could be sent through cable systems.

A fierce cable and satellite debate took place in the mid-Eighties as the BBC battled at great cost in time and manpower, involving engineers, programme producers and administrators, to solve the problem of mounting DBS. A director was appointed to deal with DBS and a possible HQ site marked out in Newcastle. By the end of 1983 it was becoming clear that the situation was critically difficult for the BBC and the implications promised to inflict real financial damage. Despite the fact that European governments were backing their own national enterprises, the British Government would not help the BBC. No public money would be made available. Almost inevitably the BBC's managers had to admit that they could not solve the problem alone, and for several months in 1984 negotiations took place with ITV and with the 'Club of 21', to which both organisations belonged and which included various commercial interests. All this came to nothing as it became clear that DBS was not a viable proposition as planned.

Reporting in the 1986 BBC Handbook, which covered events of the preceding year, the Chairman wrote of DBS that 'the commercial viability of such a service, without Government

assistance, and within the conditions established by the Government, was looking increasingly doubtful. But the BBC has every intention of remaining at the forefront of the development of new technologies serving the public interest'.

Alasdair Milne, Director-General, 1982-87

The BBC made a further attempt to play a part in the

Philips High Definition Television set

new developments by joining with a number of ITV companies that had proposed the setting up of a European Superchannel. This would, through a satellite-cable system, show programmes from the great store of British programming made by the duopoly, described by some as 'the best of British'. Transmissions began in January 1987, but severe financial problems again arose and a few months later the channel was sold to a company with quite different programming ideas.

At about the same time, the IBA was authorised by the Government to see if any group was interested in taking up the DBS challenge. Eventually, a monopoly licence was issued to British Satellite Broadcasting (BSB) which came on air in the spring of 1990 after considerable financial difficulties and technical delays. It lasted until November 1990 when it fell victim to the competition coming from Sky Channel, set up earlier by the international media entrepreneur Rupert Murdoch. BSkyB was formed from the merger. Like the BBC plans and the original Superchannel, BSB had become a casualty of the great and once promising all-British DBS cable revolution. By early 1992, however, the financial outlook for cable and satellite in Britain had improved and their share of viewing was steadily rising, affecting the audiences of both BBC and ITV.

The Radio Data System (RDS) – coded information carried on FM transmissions – enabled the BBC to introduce an improved travel service for motorists. EON (Enhanced Other Networks) receivers enable listeners to enjoy network radio and have the service interrupted if they wish by local radio travel announcements

BBC engineers had invested much time and energy in the cable and satellite debate, but had also been active in other directions. Continuing to win awards for their research work in many fields, they made important contributions in the Eighties and early Nineties to improving radio and television reception and sound reproduction. High-definition large-screen television, enhanced stereo sound and major improvements in mobile radio reception such as Radio Data System all became realities.

High Hopes and Gathering Clouds

The foreword to the BBC 1984 Handbook, written by the departing Chairman George Howard, who had been on the Board of Governors for 12 years, conveys a mixed mood of pride and apprehension, hope and mild anger. 1982-1983, the period during which the BBC celebrated its 60th anniversary in St Paul's Cathedral in the presence of the Queen, also saw the Falklands War, the start of breakfast television and further cuts in the External Services. The sense of pain and pleasure which these circumstances had produced were, unknown to the Chairman, to be exceeded in the coming five years. These would see not only the deployment of large amounts of money and manpower on the study of DBS and an unprecedented number of outside examinations of BBC finances and management, but also the emergence of some fine programmes, the winning of more prizes than ever and encouraging progress in Regional broadcasting.

Reporting the Falklands War: Brian Hanrahan

The new Director-General, Alasdair Milne, the first to come from a television production background, was for his part writing not only of the exciting future promised by the new technology but also warning of the need to 'come back from the mirages or even the glittering heights to the well-tilled and flourishing heartland'. By the heartland, he meant 'the great range of work done by network television, regional television, network radio, local radio – the absolute rock on which the organisation is built, not forgetting the world-admired service the External Services furnish in English and a variety of languages across the globe. If we ever let things go in the heartland, we would indeed have let 60 years of achievement slip. We do not intend to do that'.

The five-year period up to Milne's abrupt departure in early 1987 was marked in all the heartland areas by great programme and planning achievements. Apart from the start of the new venture, breakfast television, in January 1983, just ahead of what was to become a very tough rival, TV-am, there was a major extension of 1,000 extra hours when daytime television flourished from October 1986. Talk-shows, like breakfast television an essentially American-inspired format, had created a range of new presenters such as Michael Parkinson and

Joan Hickson as the redoubtable
Miss Marple

Alas Smith and Jones made Mel Smith and Griff Rhys Jones
into a successful duo

Michael Gambon in Dennis Potter's remarkable
The Singing Detective

Highly popular: Rowan Atkinson's *Blackadder*
spoof-history series

Madonna makes a guest appearance on
Wogan, in 1991

Russell Harty. The Eighties star was Terry Wogan who began his three programmes a week BBC1 series in 1985.

The search for individual comic talent in television continued successfully with Rowan Atkinson appearing in the highly popular spoof-history series *Blackadder*, followed by *An Alas Smith and Jones* with Mel Smith and Griff Rhys Jones; there was also the emergence of Lenny Henry and Victoria Wood. Situation comedies getting big audiences included *Allo, Allo!*, which took the unlikely subject of the French Resistance movement as its theme, and *Bread* – both of them long-running series.

The drama output was particularly interesting, with additions to the already considerable list of long-running series, serials and soap operas, such as *Miss Marple, Howards' Way* and *EastEnders,* the BBC's successful answer to Granada's *Coronation Street*. In a more thoughtful and highly original style, Alan Bennett began striking a rich seam with *An Englishman Abroad,* while Dennis Potter continued his long and successful exploration into new ways of writing television drama with his remarkable *The Singing Detective*. There began a slow decline in the number of dramatisations of classic stories but a particularly brilliant and successful example of the genre was *The Barchester Chronicles* based

'Allo 'Allo!: Broad humour from an unlikely topic

Crimewatch UK, with Sue Cook and Nick Ross, opens its files monthly

The Monocled Mutineer, with Paul McGann, caused a stir

Tumbledown, with Colin Firth

EastEnders in 1992: The BBC's successful answer to *Coronation Street*

on two of Trollope's novels. The so-called mini-series, an American concept corresponding to the popular paperbacks seen at airports, was exemplified by a bought-in programme, *The Thorn Birds,* which was compared, to the BBC's disadvantage and quite unfairly, with Granada's expensive and prestigious *Jewel in the Crown.*

This became part of what was to develop into a thorough-going BBC-bashing campaign throughout the mid-Eighties. The fact that the Corporation was producing highly stimulating and successful location dramas such as *The Boys from the Blackstuff* (commenting on unemploy-ment), *Tumbledown* (commenting on the Falklands War) and *The Monocled Mutineer* (commenting on the futility of war) added fuel to this often uncontrolled fire, fanned by some parts of the national press.

Documentary and features programmes flourished and some, such as *Timewatch* and *Crimewatch,* have stood the test of time. Major new 'blockbuster' film series – David Attenborough's *The Living Planet* and the historian John Roberts' *Triumph of the West* – received great critical acclaim, as well as attracting audiences of millions. In the 'pure' documentary field there were studies of groups of

The Paras: A documentary series

Schoolchildren using a BBC computer

professionals such as *Police* and *The Paras.* In 1982 the BBC's Natural History Unit in Bristol celebrated its 25th anniversary and produced the outstanding *Flight of the Condor.* Increasingly, feature films appeared in the schedules.

Social issues of many kinds were tackled by a wide range of departments, with charitable fund-raising being a prominent activity. July 1985 saw the 16-hour Live Aid phenomenon, broadcast by radio and television from Wembley and Philadelphia, in which numerous popular performers led by Bob Geldof joined together in a charity concert to raise money to 'feed the world'. There were apocryphal stories about the size of the worldwide audience, but it was certainly one of the largest ever amassed and over £60 million was raised. A similar but more focused production combining radio and television was made in 1985 on behalf of the annual BBC *Children in Need* appeal, which raised a record £4.5 million, a sum which was to increase to over £20 million annually by the 1990s. *Drugwatch* and *Childwatch* were other television programmes addressing increasingly worrying social problems. BBC Education mounted the innovative Computer Literacy Campaign involving the development with industry of a BBC Computer, eventually used in thousands of schools. Many campaigns concerned with social problems included radio, television and back-up services.

Radio's collaborative ventures with television represented a small part of the output of what remained a vibrant and healthy medium, despite the fall in daytime listening figures largely due to the impact of breakfast and daytime television and the arrival of commercial competition. The average listener aged four and over heard about 10.5 hours of radio in 1982 (just under half the time spent viewing television): about three-quarters of this was to BBC programmes. By 1987 the proportion of BBC listeners remained roughly the same, but the 10.5 hours had been reduced to 8.75 hours. However, there were still an average 23 million radio listeners per day in 1987 and researchers noticed the total amount of radio listening was beginning to increase. There are always fluctuations in these kind of figures at times of political crisis or major events, when listening and viewing figures rise, especially for the BBC. In 1982, for example, the Falklands War had led, over the year, to an extra 45 minutes of listening to radio per head of the population per week. Another significant factor affecting

Anthony Clare (right) sits Bruce Kent
In the Psychiatrist's Chair

Loose Ends: Saturday morning talk show, chaired by
Ned Sherrin

Phil Collins joins Mark Goodier for *Action Special –*
campaigns that are an important element of Radio 1 output

audience rating figures was the continuing expansion of BBC and ILR local radio stations, which continued to take audiences away from the BBC networks. By 1987, one-tenth of all radio listening was to BBC local radio, and car radios became much more common.

New arrivals on the radio networks which have proved to be long-running include Anthony Clare's *In the Psychiatrist's Chair,* which probes personalities in a similar but more analytical way than the *Face to Face* programmes of the Sixties, and *Loose Ends,* a fast-moving Saturday morning talk show chaired by Ned Sherrin, aimed at a younger Radio 4 audience. Radio 1 *Action Specials* were, and remain, important campaigns dealing with areas such as drugs and unemployment among young people, usually backed-up by booklets and telephone helplines. Social Action broadcasting grew rapidly with agencies such as Broadcasting Support Services providing back-up.

National and international events between 1982 and 1987 heavily engaged the news and current affairs departments in both radio and television. Several led to sharp disagreements with the Government, but the detailed coverage of the 1983 and 1987 General Elections proceeded without undue difficulty, with a Conservative win for Mrs Thatcher each time. Both involved extensive planning and organisation and were thoroughly analysed afterwards. A valuable internal account was 'The BBC's Journalism and the 1983 General Election', which considered that the campaign was generally 'dour and flat'.

A survey of the election by the BBC's Broadcasting Research Department noted how television had 'established itself in the public view as the single most authoritative and fair source of information about politics and General Election campaigns'. But, in addition, it said: 'Political campaigning has also become television-oriented, with Party Election Broadcasts of increasing sophistication and campaign "events" especially arranged for visual coverage'. A notable contribution by radio was Radio 4's daily phone-in, *Election Call,*

During the 1983 campaign, Radio 4's *Election Call* was presented by Sir Robin Day (right, with Labour's Roy Hattersley) simultaneously on BBC1

in which, during two weeks of the campaign, Sir Robin Day extensively questioned leading politicians, assisted by the electorate. It was becoming clear that, although there was much listening and viewing, the public 'felt early on in the campaign that they had heard enough about it'. On the whole, most people felt the coverage was fair, but, as this and future surveys were to show, a minority perceived a Conservative bias, a view that has, of course, been hotly denied by that party. The findings of similar research into the 1987 General Election were comparable.

In 1985, the six months' experiment of televising the House of Lords went well, but the more cautious House of Commons again voted to exclude cameras from the Chamber.

Two important episodes which involved extensive news reporting as well as considerable investment of money and manpower were the Falklands War of 1982 and the miners' strike of 1984/5. The first brought rebuke for the BBC from the Government and the Prime Minister in particular, the second complaints from the left. Both raised questions of how complex the relationship between the medium and the message was becoming, especially in political matters. In the case of a war, such as that of 1982 when the country was divided (although not nearly as much as in the Suez War), could and should the reporting be as objective and detailed as befits the aims of public service broadcasting? When reporting a strike and, in particular, a strike in which violence erupts, does the presence of reporters and, especially, cameras, affect events?

The practical difficulties of reporting a distant war were immense, and to obtain and transmit television pictures posed major logistical problems, which led to arguments with the Ministry of Defence. Mrs Thatcher accused the BBC of not presenting the British case (ie, the Government's case) vigorously enough and resented the use of Argentinian film, which was plentiful. The Chairman and Director-General suffered an unpleasant grilling at the hands of the Conservative Backbench Media Committee on 13 May, after a *Panorama* programme which looked at the views of those who had doubts about the Falklands campaign. Accusations of lack of patriotism were made both at the meeting and in parts of the tabloid press, but calmer opinion knew the inaccuracy of such accusations. The public turned predominantly to the BBC, as it usually does on such important national occasions, and research showed that audiences took, again as they usually do, a more relaxed view of the arguments about bias in reporting. As the campaign developed, the BBC's editorial even-handedness was questioned but, overall, there was a high degree of public support with eight in 10 people believing the BBC had behaved responsibly.

Until the late Seventies, there had been a healthy although sometimes wary relationship between the trade-union movement and the broadcasters. However, well before the miners' strike began in March 1984, a spate of books, research reports and studies claimed anti-union and anti-working-class bias in media reporting, the BBC often being cited as culpable. A BBC study of the events observed that: 'The miners' strike of 1984/5 was a unique event: in its length, the intensity of the passion it aroused, in the profound effect it had on many communities and, not least, in the challenges it offered those who sought to report, analyse and interpret it'. The violence that followed, both between the police and strikers and between the broadcasters and strikers, was particularly worrying. As the BBC Handbook noted, in a year in which the 'news machine' had been tested to the full, the miners' strike had received 'more coverage than any other in the history of British broadcasting'. The BBC's ability to remain balanced and impartial was tested, because, just as those on the left saw the BBC as the 'Establishment' in action, so those on the right perceived partiality towards the miners. It was with some world-weariness that, in the year following the strike, the BBC received a particularly violent charge of anti-Government bias from Norman Tebbit, the Conservative Party Chairman, over the reporting of a major international story in Libya. The BBC vigorously showed that the charges were unjust, but it looked as if a concerted campaign was under way to destabilise it at the very least. Others took the view that the BBC was getting careless.

This difference of perception was reinforced by conflicts of opinion over some current affairs documentaries produced between 1984 and 1986. *Maggie's Militant Tendency* was a *Panorama* programme transmitted in January 1984, which attempted to examine what were claimed to be the far-right views of some members of the Conservative Party, and was originally based on material supplied by some young

After *At the Edge of the Union* was transmitted, the public wondered what the fuss had been about

Conservatives. After much argument about the facts presented and the validity of the research put into the preparation of the programme, libel claims by two Conservative MPs were settled in the High Court in October 1986 with the payment of damages by the BBC.

Raising more fundamental questions for the BBC itself was a 1985 programme in the *Real Lives* series called *At the Edge of the Union*, as this provoked major internal differences, always a dangerous development. The series looked at the lives of various individuals in some depth; this particular edition was concerned with two men at the extremes of the political divide in Northern Ireland. One was said to be a leading IRA figure. In a speech on 15 July the Prime Minister had made it plain that she felt that terrorists should be denied 'the oxygen of publicity', and later in July the Home Secretary, Leon Brittan, in his capacity as the Minister concerned with security, wrote to the BBC Chairman at that time, Stuart Young, prior to the planned transmission of the programme in August, asking that it should not be broadcast. He had not seen the programme and his action seemed to call into question the BBC's independence. After much internal debate and disagreement between the Board of Governors (who viewed the programme and disliked it) and Management (who wished to show it), the transmission was cancelled. A 24-hour strike by BBC and ITN journalists took place. Some small changes and additions to the programme were eventually made and, following strenuous pleas from Alasdair Milne, it was broadcast in October. The public and many critics wondered what all the fuss had been about.

A third contentious programme was one of a six-part television series called *Secret Society*, produced in Scotland. It concerned another subject, security, which was and remains an issue of major public controversy and, like Northern Ireland, Mrs Thatcher felt passionately about it. The *Spycatcher* book affair brought it into special prominence.

The programme concerned the alleged existence of a secret Government plan to build a spy satellite, Zircon. Before it could be shown, the BBC headquarters in Glasgow were raided on 31 January 1987 and over 30 boxes of programme material and videotapes were removed by the police. There was uproar in Parliament and the press following this unprecedented action. The new Chairman of the BBC, Marmaduke Hussey, protested strongly. He had taken up his appointment in November after the death of Stuart Young in August 1986, following an interregnum during which the newly appointed Vice-Chairman, Lord Barnett, had acted as Chairman. The Zircon incident was dramatic enough, but it had been preceded on 29 January by the departure of the Director-General, Alasdair Milne. This followed a meeting between him, the Chairman and the Vice-Chairman who said that the Board of Governors wished to make major changes in the running of the BBC, which would clearly involve changes at the top. Alasdair Milne's resignation was requested and he resigned that day. The Corporation was in an unprecedented state of embattlement and turmoil.

It would take considerable skill to solve the problems the BBC faced, which were not only concerned with new technology and contentious programmes. Clearly, the Government intended to make fundamental changes to the whole of the UK broadcasting system. Not only had numerous studies of BBC finances and management methods been instituted over recent years but a Committee on Financing the BBC, under the chairmanship of a distinguished economist, Sir Alan Peacock, had been set up in 1985 with a limited remit. Starting work in May, it had reported by July the following year.

It was well known that the Prime Minister did not like the licence fee as a means of financing the BBC, regarding it as a kind of poll tax. The task of the Peacock Committee was 'To assess the effects of the introduction of advertising or sponsorship on the BBC's Home Services, either as an alternative or a supplement to the monies now received though the licence fee...' and to determine the effects of such a move on independent broadcasting, cable and satellite services. Other ways of raising money were also to be looked at. In the meantime the licence fee settlement of 1981 had to be renegotiated. As part of its preparation, the BBC in 1984 engaged a firm of accountants, Peat Marwick Mitchell, to assess the value for money offered by the licence fee. At $12\frac{1}{2}$p per day for all its services, or 2p per television viewing hour per average viewer, it appeared very good value. Most of the recommendations made by Peat Marwick Mitchell were taken up but the episode sparked off a vigorous debate, particularly in the press. The question of the break-up of the BBC and the sale of its constituent parts became a live issue, encouraged in 1985 by a series of critical leading articles in *The Times*.

Peacock's report was radical and, in some ways, surprising. Somewhat to the Government's dismay, it rejected supplementing the licence fee by advertising, although in the longer term the idea of subscription funding found favour.

ctor-General, Sir Michael Checkland,
at White City

Chairman, Marmaduke Hussey, at
Broadcasting House

Partnership with Change

The years from 1987 to 1992 witnessed the most radical changes ever seen in broadcasting in the United Kingdom. To a very large extent, these reflected worldwide events, as well as Government policies. Almost everywhere in the developed world, commercial broadcasting through cable, satellite and terrestrial channels flourished while public sector broadcasting went on the defensive. The BBC, generally recognised to be the biggest and most successful example of the latter, could not alone expect to escape major changes. Under its new management it resolved to welcome the new climate and to strengthen its position in every possible way, competing with what were to be an increasing number of operators at home and abroad. Since it had to do this with a declining real income and during what was to develop into the worst recession since the Thirties, the necessary decisions were bound to be difficult. The process of shedding permanent staff, a major cost factor, would need to speed up. Michael Checkland and his colleagues set about devising a five-year plan to cover the years 1988/93, which would ultimately prepare the BBC for the negotiations leading up to Charter Renewal in 1996.

Change had begun with a radical management restructuring. Apart from the appointment of the new Director-General in February, John Birt, Director of Programmes at London Weekend Television, had been invited soon afterwards to become Deputy Director-General, with a special remit to reappraise and supervise the BBC's journalism. New appointments were made to two of the three Managing Director posts, in Radio and the External Services (renamed BBC World Service in September 1988), and the structure of non-metropolitan broadcasting was radically changed in

Two recommendations, however, had a fairly rapid effect. The licence fee from 1988 was to be pegged to the Retail Price Index (RPI) and both the BBC and ITV would have to guarantee that a proportion of their transmitted programmes would be made by independent producers.

Since the level of licence fee settlement of £58 in 1985 was below that asked for (£65) and since broadcasting costs were known to run ahead of RPI, the first of these represented a tough 'double squeeze', in the words of the Home Secretary, Douglas Hurd, speaking in January 1987. The second presented considerable planning and resource problems and led to cuts in BBC staff levels which, in the early Eighties, reached their maximum of around 30,000. It was as well that the new Director-General, Michael Checkland, had been for many years the Corporation's expert in financial and resource matters, as well as Deputy Director-General under Alasdair Milne.

June 1987 with the appointment, for the first time, of a Managing Director Regional Broadcasting. The pace of change grew rapidly. In 1991, the Chairman, Marmaduke Hussey, was able to report: 'The BBC has much altered since 1986. The entire management has changed with the sole exception of our able Managing Director of the World Service, John Tusa. With this exception, most of the top jobs are now held by different people, including an influx, but in my view still too small, of people from outside the organisation'.

The process of planning change took place against a broadcasting landscape which was itself rapidly altering. In February 1987, the Government issued a consultative document called 'Radio Choices and Opportunities', which sought to find ways of offering more listening choice without damaging public service broadcasting, exemplified by the BBC. New VHF frequencies, available under international agreements, meant that there was scope for new national and local services including 'community or special interest radio stations'. Earlier attempts to set up community radio had failed. Most important for the BBC was the possibility of new national services run on a commercial basis and with a lighter regulatory touch. As the new stations came on air without the obligation placed on public service broadcasters to supply a wide range of programming, how would BBC Radio resist the temptation to go downmarket in efforts to retain its share of the audience? The difficult question of the sustainability of the licence fee in such circumstances became more urgent. Ideological and business opponents of the BBC missed no opportunity to press home their message.

A Cabinet Committee chaired by the Prime Minister met throughout 1987 to consider how the Government, re-elected in June of that year, was to move towards a full-blown Broadcasting Bill, eventually produced in December 1989. Meanwhile the broad directions were becoming clear in the light of the Peacock Report and the consultative paper on radio. There was to be a huge expansion of both radio and television channels, together with an increase in independent production from companies outside the duopoly. Peacock had recommended a 40% increase in such production in television over 10 years but, after negotiations with the Home Secretary, Douglas Hurd, it was agreed that 25% of output, excluding news, should be made in this way from 1993. Although by September 1987 much of the detail of the Government's proposals was not clear, Mrs Thatcher's general attitudes were. At a special seminar held in Downing Street in that month, she described broadcasting as 'one of the last bastions of restrictive practices'.

Bearing in mind a promise in the Conservative Election Manifesto to act on the question of sex and violence, perceived by some to be treated carelessly, the Home Secretary in October proposed the setting up of the Broadcasting Standards Council. This was to consider complaints from the public, institute research, monitor standards and keep the public informed. The Council began work in 1988, with some criticism being made that the Government was setting up yet another supervisory body alongside the Broadcasting Complaints Commission at a time when a 'light touch' was stated policy. These criticisms grew as investigations, edicts and new broadcasting legislation increased in the Eighties.

The political restrictions on broadcasters were made plain in a number of instances and there were sharp divisions over

nifer Saunders and Dawn French broke into the top
ranks of television comics

Fortunes of War, with Kenneth Branagh and
Emma Thompson

ers: Gives listeners the opportunity
to air their causes

Children in Need in 1991, with
Sue Cook and Terry Wogan

the justification for the Government's actions in each. During the *Spycatcher* case, a three-part series had been prepared in 1987 by Radio News and Current Affairs called *My Country: Right or Wrong,* examining the work of the security services. Despite careful research and official clearances, the transmissions were halted by an injunction sought by the Government on the grounds that confidentiality and possibly security might have been breached. Such fears proved to be unfounded, the injunction on all three programmes was lifted by June 1988 and the series broadcast six months late.

In that year there were two other events which illustrated the difficulties faced by all broadcasters in reporting events in Northern Ireland. A major controversy arose in March over the showing of a documentary, *Death on the Rock,* made by Thames Television. This investigated the circumstances surrounding the shooting of three IRA terrorists in Gibraltar and which the Home Office had requested should not be shown. Despite being exonerated later by an independent committee chaired by a distinguished Conservative politician, Lord Windlesham, the programme and its producers attracted the intense wrath of the Government. This spread to other broadcasters dealing with sensitive and difficult programme matters like the coverage in Northern Ireland. Later in the year the Government placed restrictions on broadcasting interviews with terrorists and members of organisations supporting terrorism in Northern Ireland. One consequence was to confine interviews with the legal party Sinn Fein to pictures of interviewees without the soundtrack, but with either a dubbed voice or superimposed words. Both the BBC and IBA sought unsuccessfully to have this restriction lifted.

While these disputes caught the headlines, there were other less sensational but more positive events taking place. In 1987 the BBC had joined with ITV in an anti-Aids campaign; French and Saunders had joined the ranks of successful female television comics; *Fortunes of War* had been a great success in drama; *Punters* had opened up new possibilities for radio listeners to air their own causes; and the *Children in Need* appeal reached about £14 million. After a four-day conference in July 1987 the Deputy

Children's drama at its best: *The Lion, the Witch and the Wardrobe*, part of *The Chronicles of Narnia* cycle

Almost 18 million people watched *Elizabeth R*: The documentary filmed over 12 months in celebration of the Queen's 40th anniversary of her accession to the throne

Director-General announced that a combined News and Current Affairs Directorate would be set up covering both radio and television. This evidently sensible and straightforward rationalisation had been the subject of much disagreement and contention over the years.

In January 1988 the *See for Yourself* accountability campaign, involving radio and television programmes nationally, regionally and locally, sought to create a forum in which the BBC explained itself directly to the public, and senior managers were questioned live on-air by licence-payers. *Def II* opened up a new strand of television programming for young adults and *The Chronicles of Narnia* added new glories to children's drama. Another important development was the start of work on a large new building in White City to replace expensive leased

properties in central London and, in the words of the Board of Governors' review of the year, 'budgeting flesh was put on the bones of the five-year plan' which had been announced in November 1987.

With efficiency as its major theme, the BBC plan, as set out in a document distributed widely to staff, was 'to maintain and improve the range and diversity of its programmes, ensuring these are made to the highest standards'. Detailed work began in all directorates immediately, but several new important initiatives were already to be seen in outline. Some of these had painful implications such as the commitment to reduce staff costs in all areas, completion of the local radio network at the expense of 10% savings in operating costs and a substantial move towards independent production, with all that would entail for in-house services. Further measures to ensure that the Corporation would survive robustly on a reduced real income each year included a pledge to increase BBC Enterprises' turnover and to launch what were then referred to as 'night-time downloading services'. This scheme involved the exploitation of the BBC2 transmitter network outside normal hours, initially to transmit programmes to doctors on a subscription basis, using automatic video-recording during the night. After overcoming some early difficulties, including the start of the recession, the scheme developed in 1992 into BBC Select, offering a range of training and education programmes to a wider selection of special interest groups. Niche (highly targeted) programming and the use of scrambled and decoded signals became part of an entirely new BBC service involving sponsorship, advertising and commercial partnerships.

The White Paper of November 1988, entitled 'Broadcasting in the 90s: Competition, Choice and Quality', was a major document containing the Government's thoughts on the likely direction of a future Broadcasting Bill, eventually published a year later. Some critics thought that the three words of the subtitle were in precisely the wrong order. It led to a long debate on many fundamental topics, particularly about what was meant by quality and choice in the new broadcasting era and how unfettered the proposed competition was likely to be. The main subject of the White Paper was reform in the independent sector of the duopoly, the assumption being that changes to the BBC would come later as 1996, the date for the renewal of its Royal Charter, approached. However, the BBC was much encouraged by the White Paper's confirmation of its position as 'the cornerstone of British broadcasting'.

When the Broadcasting Bill finally appeared, after much debate, arguing and special pleading, its central intention was to change drastically the way in which commercial broadcasting licences were awarded, by introducing the 'highest bidder' principle. This proposal, much criticised on all sides, was modified but not sufficiently to save it from almost universal disapproval. A new authority called the Independent Television Commission would replace the IBA and a separate Radio Authority set up. There would be many more radio and television channels and the Broadcasting Standards Council was given statutory 'bite'.

Apart from the arrival of greatly increased competition, which would expand even more in the mid-Nineties, there were two major implications for the BBC. The Office of Fair Trading was added to the already long list of supervisory bodies in broadcasting – monitoring the 25% quota of commissions to be awarded to independent producers – and there was an intention to remove the protection given to the BBC and ITV which guaranteed them access to 10 listed sporting events. This could mean that national occasions such as Test Match cricket or Wimbledon might be available only to those who could afford to acquire satellite or cable television. The fact that cable operators would not be required to carry BBC and ITV/Channel 4 signals underlined the deprivation which would ensue in the name of unregulated competition. The cable and satellite operators were naturally delighted and accused the BBC and ITV of living in the past.

The members of the duopoly were soon to lose another privilege, that of owning the exclusive copyright in weekly programme listings. The result of that was a decline in the circulation of *Radio Times* and *TV Times* and a loss of income as other listings magazines entered the marketplace. Another indication of increased competition in the publishing side of broadcasting was the decision to close *The Listener* in January 1991 despite attempts to save it in its last years by publishing it jointly with ITV. With heavy annual losses no longer sustainable at a time of financial constraints, the only magazine which reflected in print the range of quality programmes made by the BBC came to an end after 62 years.

Hostages returning from Kuwait thank the World Service's *Gulf Link* programme for keeping them in touch with home

Director-General Michael Checkland (second left, back) and Rolf Seelmann-Eggebert, Chairman of One World group of broadcasters (third left, back) with key contributors

Historic reporting: Kate Adie in Peking

Notable drama: *Oranges Are Not the Only Fruit*, with Charlotte Coleman and Geraldine McEwan

As the Eighties closed and the Nineties began, the tasks facing programme-makers in news and current affairs became particularly challenging, with the momentous events in China and Eastern Europe being followed by the Gulf War. BBC correspondents provided distinguished coverage of these landmark changes with viewers able instantly to see historic images from the Berlin Wall, Tiananmen Square, Romania, the Soviet Union and Kuwait.

At home, the experiment in televising the House of Commons in 1989 proved successful and on 19 July 1990 MPs voted for the cameras to stay. The BBC had played an important part in the whole episode and, despite the fact that an independent company was in overall charge, it was now able to consolidate its entire Westminster operation in new premises. Other signs of a new climate were the BBC's transmission of Granada's *What the Papers Say* in 1989 and various agreements made with cable and satellite operators. The Director-General continually emphasised the BBC's positive attitude towards 'entering the new age of broadcasting'.

Programme-makers continued to provide excellent entertainment and new ideas. Notable television dramas of the period were *Oranges Are Not the Only Fruit, Portrait of a Marriage* and *House of Cards*, the latter being an example of a popular new genre, the political thriller. The *One World* project, a collaborative venture involving a consortium of European broadcasters including the BBC, was concerned

Sir David Attenborough's *The Trials of Life:*
An example of Regional Broadcasting's
contribution to national television

The Late Show logo

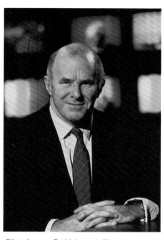

Clive James: Satirising satellite

with the planet's environmental problems and was seen in over 20 countries. Sir David Attenborough's *Trials of Life* was the major documentary achievement of the year and a fine example of work coming from Regional Broadcasting, in this case the South and West. 35% of BBC1 and BBC2 programmes now originated in the regions. *The Late Show*, BBC2's flagship arts programme, won an award for innovation from the British Film Institute, and Clive James in *Saturday Night Clive* enjoyed himself and entertained viewers by satirising the new satellite stations. Numerous long-running popular series such as *Only Fools and Horses* and *The Generation Game* continued to attract huge audiences – viewing figures in 1990/91 were around 17 million. With *EastEnders* attracting 19 million and the bought-in series *Neighbours* 16 million, the BBC was able to hold its audience share at around 48%. Because of the increased competition from commercial stations, BBC Radio reviewed its networks with a view to holding as much as possible of its

65% audience share. The major innovation was the opening of Radio 5 in August 1990, designed chiefly to carry education, youth and sports programmes, with a selection of World Service output.

With the Broadcasting Act expected to receive the Royal Assent at the end of 1990, the licence fee due to be pegged below RPI from April 1991 and with a recent industrial dispute over a pay claim, prompt action was required on financing. 'Funding the Future', approved in January 1990, was the report of a BBC internal committee set up to consider savings that could bring pay more in line with the commercial sector without affecting programme quality. Among the range of proposals in the report were cut-backs in the White City site plan, a reduction in the number of English regions from five to four and a greater use of outside support services, intended to save staff costs. By 1991 the implementation of these measures, together with

Caroline Mardon

Continuing to set the political agenda:
Brian Redhead, one of Radio 4's
Today team

Kenneth Branagh's *Hamlet*, heard on Radio 3

BBC Radio Berkshire was the last of the 39 local radio
stations to open in England. Pictured here: Howard
Hughes, Radio Berkshire's morning presenter

Scotland's comic philosopher: Rab C. Nesbitt

Radio 5 presenter, Danny Baker

Gloria Hunniford on Radio 2

One of the first full-facility television
studio cameras used in the BBC

Music Course on School Radio

natural wastage and retraining, had led to savings of some £80 million, the extra money not only going towards better pay but also towards programme enhancement.

Together with other new policies, such as those resulting from increasing independent production, the effect of these decisions also led to a reduction of 4,000 staff in the Home Services. A further major new step, Producer Choice, was announced in October 1991. Because of the legal necessity to commission a quarter of BBC television programmes from independent producers by 1993/94, there would clearly be a reduced demand for internal resources such as film crews, studios and post-production facilities. In time, property housing these facilities would have to be given up. By allocating cash budgets to programme-makers, Producer Choice plans to allow them to buy the necessary resources either outside the BBC or to use in-house facilities to get the best value for money. Equally, internal departments supplying resources will be funded entirely by selling their services to producers. Internal pricing would be created and plans were quickly put in place to ensure the full implementation of this radical new approach to production by April 1993. An inevitable consequence of Producer Choice was a thorough review of all the BBC's overheads, deemed to absorb too large a percentage of the licence income. The Overheads Review in 1992 closely examined all areas of the BBC not directly involved in making programmes and a range of cuts was proposed. These new policies set up a vigorous debate among producers, resource departments and support services. How much money would be saved? Would the system avoid creating a new layer of financial administration? What would be the effect on programme quality? How is a support service defined and would the advantages of the BBC's size be lost?

As the BBC approached its 70th anniversary, it was announced in July 1991 that the Deputy Director-General, John Birt, would become Director-General in early 1993 and lead the BBC through the Charter Renewal process and into the period beyond that. From now on, the spotlight would be turned on the BBC, as the Government made plain. An important element in the lengthy process of self-reappraisal had already begun in March 1991 when 15 task forces, consisting of about 120 members of middle management, began their work of considering the role of the BBC in the new multi-channel environment. Their job was to consider aspects of many BBC activities, from output areas such as children's programmes and news to the Corporation's role internationally and as an entrepreneur. The consultants McKinsey were engaged to help guide the exercise, which was designed to produce as wide a range of fresh ideas as possible. Their detailed reports were passed to the Charter review group to draft into a BBC document to form the basis of a wide-ranging public debate, along with the Government's Green Paper on the BBC.

The Corporation was preparing itself for the most important decisions to be taken about its future since John Reith set about tackling similar problems 70 years earlier. His foresight then, when very early in his BBC career he had proposed an Empire Service, was again about to be proved justified as global communication rose to the top of the Corporation's agenda.

Global Communications

Speaking at the opening of the BBC's Empire Service in 1932, Sir John Reith said that radio was 'an instrument of almost incalculable importance in the social and political life of the community. Its influence will more and more be felt in the daily life of the individual in almost every sphere of human activity, in affairs national and international.' The ambition to set up what was one of the first external broadcasting services in the world had formed in his mind soon after he arrived at the BBC, but it took nearly 10 years to turn his vision into reality. Another visionary, the Canadian literary critic and sociologist Marshall McLuhan, who wrote so originally about the nature of new communication media in the Sixties, observed: 'The new electronic interdependence recreates the world in the image of a global village.'

Lynette Lithgow in the BBC World Service Television News studio

The BBC World Service, which grew from the Empire Service, and which celebrated its 60th anniversary in 1992, made particularly important contributions to the notion of global communication between 1987 and 1992, although one might question if 'village' is an appropriate image for the large and diverse community it serves. Its audience in that community, listening in English and 36 other languages, is estimated to be 120 million, making the BBC the largest international broadcaster in the world in audience terms and, in terms of hours transmitted, Europe's largest and fourth in the world. In the same five-year period, the World Service increased its broadcast hours by nearly 100 per week, or 14%, and its grant-in-aid income from the Government by 6% in real terms. The financial arrangements of the BBC's external broadcasting had been greatly improved in 1985 when its income for the first time was arranged on a three-yearly rather than yearly basis, so allowing for better planning.

International recognition of the Service was greatly enhanced when Mikhail Gorbachev and Terry Waite both paid remarkable tributes to it in 1991. Both had learned the truth about world events listening to the BBC World Service while enduring two quite different forms of imprisonment.

It was a natural ambition for the BBC to create a television equivalent of its international radio service. In March 1991, this ambition was achieved when the first 30-minute nightly bulletin of BBC World Service Television news was transmitted to Europe by satellite as part of a subscription satellite channel, BBC TV Europe. A wholly owned self-funding subsidiary of the BBC called BBC World Service Television Ltd. was created in April 1991 and in October it extended its operation into Asia through an agreement with a Hong Kong commercial enterprise. This company provides the capital and marketing skills for running a multi-channel operation, one of which is World Service Television. It also inserts the advertisements which support the operation. World Service Radio is funded by a grant-in-aid; World Service Television

Terry Waite, who was sustained by listening to the World Service during captivity in the Lebanon, appears on *Outlook* after his release

receives no revenue from this source or from the TV licence fee. The BBC has full editorial control of the news bulletins compiled in London for its worldwide audience which can pick up the signals with a satellite dish direct into the home or through cable systems. From 15 November 1991 World Service Television was running a 24-hour news operation.

Step-by-step this service has been extended, first to the Middle East and then to Africa where, from April 1992, many more million people were able to view BBC news. By the end of 1993 BBC World Service Television is aiming to be global.

This remarkable achievement is a fine illustration of the BBC's ability to innovate and adapt to the new, competitive climate in which the international dimension becomes increasingly important. We not only expect to send and receive programmes to and from all parts of the earth: the ownership of broadcasting systems is transnational, co-productions seek to satisfy more than one culture, rules about taste and technology are governed by international agreements. The major question becomes: 'For what purpose is all this global communication being designed?' The BBC, with its public service ethos, is in a strong position to assert the primary need, which is to tell the truth. Other broadcasting systems in different parts of the world have different priorities, some political, some commercial.

ing its licence income. Aware of the rapid expansion of satellite and cable and its potential size in the late Nineties, the BBC also linked up with commercial companies like Thames Television and BSkyB to plan and launch specialist satellite channels, funded by a combination of subscription and advertising. The BBC's unique archive of programme material and the breadth of its news and current affairs are valuable resources which will be exploited in the new media to increase the BBC's revenue outside the licence fee.

In 1923, John Reith, although well aware of political realities and not opposed to commercial advertising, was struggling to create an organisation which he wished to be free from the domination of both politicians and businessmen, the two great power-brokers. He was already seeking ways of persuading the Government to help create broadcasting organisations in India and other parts of the Empire. It was not until 1932 that he achieved his international goal. In his diary he wrote: 'There is neither vision nor recognition of the immense potentialities of broadcasting: no ethical or moral appreciation; just commercialism.' Reith's aim was to broadcast truth in the service of the whole of the population and to oppose profit-making and power-seeking as the principal reasons for setting up broadcasting stations. In 1924, he defined the BBC's purpose: 'To bring the best of everything to the greatest number of homes'.

The growth of World Service Television was accompanied in 1992 by other important developments, highlighting the future shape of broadcasting in Britain and the BBC's commitment to supplement-

Some of Reith's legacy has, over the last 70 years, had to be modified, but, surely, these aspirations still incorporate the essential elements of the public service broadcasting ethic.

A 9-metre dish installed at Television Centre in 1991, for reception and transmission of satellite signals

Date list

A programme entry, in italics, shows the date of a first transmission with (R) for radio and (T) for television. All 'firsts' refer to BBC programmes. Dates relating to Royal Charters, Chairmen, Directors-General, Governments and Ministers and Committees of Enquiry will be found on the Chart inserted inside the back cover.

1922

18 Oct British Broadcasting Company Ltd formed
1 Nov Broadcasting Licence Fee of 10 shillings introduced
14 Nov First daily transmission from 2LO
15 Nov First broadcasts from Birmingham and Manchester
14 Dec John Reith made General Manager of BBC
23 Dec First orchestral concert, regular General News bulletin from London, talk and dance music
24 Dec First play written for radio and first religious address

1923

8 Jan First outside broadcast
18 Jan Licence from Postmaster-General issued to British Broadcasting Company Ltd
30 Jan First variety programme
17 Feb First broadcast appeal
22 Feb First broadcast debate
26 Mar First daily weather forecast
29 Apr First SOS message
1 May Savoy Hill Studios opened. Evening talks for men started
2 May First afternoon talk for women
28 May First full-length play
29 Aug First simultaneous broadcast of news over all stations
28 Sept *Radio Times* first published
8 Nov First broadcast in Welsh from Cardiff
26 Nov First experimental broadcast to America
2 Dec First broadcast in Gaelic from Aberdeen
30 Dec First continental programme relayed by landline

1924

6 Jan First religious service
5 Feb First Greenwich Time Signal
17 Feb First Big Ben daily time signal

4 Apr First national schools broadcast
23 Apr First broadcast by King George V
19 May Song of nightingale broadcast from a Surrey wood with cello accompaniment
12 Jun First disc-jockey programme
13 Oct First broadcast election address (by the Prime Minister, Ramsay MacDonald)
10 Nov First running commentary (Lord Mayor's Show)
26 Nov First relay from America

1925

19 Feb First broadcast for farmers (market prices)
6 Apr 2LO transmitter moved from Marconi House to roof of Selfridges
27 Jul Daventry transmitter 5XX opened

1926

24 Jan *The Week's Good Cause* (R)
4-12 May General Strike
26 Sept *Epilogue* (R)
26 Oct First theatre organ broadcast
31 Dec British Broadcasting Company dissolved

1927

1 Jan British Broadcasting Corporation established by Royal Charter
4 Jan First meeting of Board of Governors
15 Jan First running commentary on a Rugby International match under new arrangement with the press. Followed in the spring and summer by first commentaries on Association Football, Grand National, Oxford and Cambridge Boat Race, FA Cup Final, cricket, Royal Tournament, Trooping the Colour and Wimbledon tennis
13 Aug First BBC Prom from Queen's Hall
11 Nov Experimental broadcast to Empire from Chelmsford

1928

2 Jan Regular weekday Religious Service began
5 Mar Ban on controversial broadcasts lifted
12 Mar First broadcast by BBC Dance Orchestra (Jack Payne)
25 Apr First Budget broadcast (Winston Churchill)

1929

16 Jan *The Listener* first published
19 Jul *Toytown* (R)
20 Aug First BBC transmission of 30-line experimental television using Baird's studio
6 Nov *Week in Parliament* (R), later called *Week in Westminster*

1930

10 Feb BBC began editing news bulletins with newly acquired news agency tape machines
9 Mar Start of Regional Scheme offering alternative radio programmes
14 Jul First experimental television play *The Man With a Flower in his Mouth*
22 Oct First broadcast by BBC Symphony Orchestra

1931

9 May Mr Middleton's first gardening broadcast
27 Jul First broadcast of BBC Theatre Orchestra
18 Dec First broadcast of BBC Chamber Orchestra

1932

12 Mar First broadcast from Broadcasting House
26 Mar *Music Hall* (R)
1 May Broadcasting House became BBC HQ
14 May *The End of Savoy Hill* (R)
19 Jun First service broadcast from All Souls, Langham Place
22 Aug First experimental television programme broadcast from Broadcasting House
19 Dec Short-wave Empire Service from Daventry inaugurated
25 Dec First Empire Christmas Day programme and message from King George V

1933

16 Jun First broadcast programme of BBC Organ from Concert Hall, Broadcasting House
28 Jul First female radio announcer (Sheila Barrett)
18 Nov *In Town Tonight* (R)
11 Dec *Scrapbook for 1913* (R) First in series

1934

15 Jan Commercially sponsored programmes began from Radio Luxembourg aimed at Britain
7 Oct Droitwich high-power long-wave transmitter replaced Daventry 5XX
29 Nov First broadcast of a Royal wedding, with world coverage (Duke of Kent and Princess Marina)

1935

6 Apr *The American Half Hour* (R) Alistair Cooke

1936

20 Jan John Reith announced the death of King George V
28 Feb *The March of the '45* – a notable feature programme
29 May First broadcast from Glyndebourne
31 Aug First female television announcer (Elixabeth Cowell)
1 Oct BBC Staff Training and Listener Research Sections formed
2 Nov Official inauguration of world's first regular high-definition television service from Alexandra Palace
9 Nov *Picture Page* (T)
21 Nov Mr Middleton's first television broadcast on gardening
8 Dec First complete ballet televised
9 Dec First televised cookery demonstration
11 Dec King Edward VIII's Abdication broadcast from Windsor Castle, announced by John Reith

1937

5 Apr *Monday at Seven* (R), later called *Monday Night at Eight*
12 May Coronation of King George VI and Queen Elizabeth (R & T). First use of television outside broadcast van
21 Jun Wimbledon tennis (T)
20 Jul Death of Marconi

1938

3 Jan First BBC foreign-language service (Arabic)
5 Jan *Band Waggon* (R)
15 Mar Latin American Service began
21 Mar Television included news for first time (recording of radio news, no pictures)
2 Apr Oxford and Cambridge Boat Race (T)
30 Apr FA Cup Final from Wembley (T)
9 Jun Trooping the Colour (T)
30 Jun John Reith resigned
27 Sept Start of European Service with news in French, German and Italian
30 Sept Chamberlain's return from Munich meeting with Hitler broadcast live on radio and television

1939

18 Apr First broadcast of English lesson (in Arabic Service)
12 Jul *ITMA* (R) with Tommy Handley
1 Aug First broadcast to Europe in English
23 Aug *London Calling* first published
26 Aug BBC Monitoring Service began
1 Sept TV Service closed down. Home Service replaced National and Regional programmes
3 Sept Chamberlain and King George VI broadcast on declaration of war (R)
1 Oct First wartime broadcast by Winston Churchill
10 Nov *Garrison Theatre* (R) with Jack Warner

1940

7 Jan Forces Programme began
19 May Churchill's first broadcast as Prime Minister
26 May *Hi, Gang!* (R)
5 Jun J.B. Priestley's first *Postscript* to the news
18 Jun Churchill's 'This was their finest hour' broadcast. De Gaulle's first broadcast to France
23 Jun *Music While You Work* (R)
7 Jul *Radio Newsreel* (R) in the European Service
25 Sept St George's Hall gutted by incendiary bombs
15 Oct Bomb exploded in Broadcasting House during 9 o'clock news: 7 deaths
19 Nov Transmitter in Birmingham destroyed by bombs
8 Dec Broadcasting House badly damaged by land-mine

1941

1 Jan *The Brains Trust* (R), originally called *Any Questions?*
14 Jan Belgian Service began 'V' campaign
21 Feb BBC premises in Swansea destroyed by bombs
17 Mar European Service moved to Bush House
10 May Queen's Hall demolished by bombs. Maida Vale and other BBC premises badly damaged
31 May *Workers' Playtime* (R)
6 Jul *London Calling Europe (*R) in English
9 Nov *Sincerely Yours, Vera Lynn* (R)
21 Dec *The Man Born to be King* (R)

1942

29 Jan *Desert Island Discs* (R)
22 Mar First daily news bulletin in Morse code for the Resistance in Europe
6 May *The Radio Doctor* (R) Charles Hill

1943

3 Apr *Saturday-Night Theatre* (R)
13 Jun Overseas Forces Programme became General Overseas Service. Empire Service became Overseas Service
4 Jul *English by Radio* for Europe
11 Jul Broadcast for clandestine European Press began

1944

10 Feb Beginning of self-imposed 14-Day Rule
27 Feb *Variety Bandbox* (R)
6 Jun D-Day – *War Report* (R)
7 Jun Allied Expeditionary Forces Programme began
30 Jun Flying-bomb damage to Bush House

1945

15 Feb First Commonwealth Broadcast Conference opened in London
8 May Broadcast by Churchill and King George VI on VE-Day
29 Jul Regional broadcasts renewed and Light Programme began
1 Aug *Family Favourites* (R)
15 Aug Broadcasts by Attlee and King George VI on VJ-Day
3 Sept Forces Educational Broadcasts began
1 Oct *World Theatre* (R)
9 Oct *Today in Parliament* (R)

1946

4 Mar *Housewives' Choice* (R)
Have A Go (R) Wilfred Pickles from North Region, later networked
24 Mar *Letter from America* (R)
7 Jun Television Service resumed on 405 lines
8 Jun Victory Parade televised
7 Jul *For the Children* (T) First television for children
19 Aug *Mr Pastry* (T) Richard Hearne
15 Sept First religious service televised
29 Sept Third Programme began
4 Oct *From Our Own Correspondent* (R)
7 Oct *Woman's Hour* (R)
Dick Barton, Special Agent (R)
20 Oct *Muffin the Mule* (T)
29 Dec *Down Your Way* (R)

1947

2 Jan *Much Binding in the Marsh* (R)

9 Feb Home Service and Light Programme closed early due to fuel crisis
10 Feb Third Programme and Television Service suspended
26 Feb Third Programme resumed
28 Feb *Twenty Questions* (R)
11 Mar Television Service resumed
18 Mar First radio Party Political Broadcast (Prime Minister Attlee)
9 Apr *How Does Your Garden Grow?* (R) from the North Region. Became *Gardeners' Question Time* in 1951
13 Sept *Last Night of the Proms* (T)
28 Sept *The Critics* (R)
2 Nov *Round Britain Quiz* (R)
6 Nov *Designed for Women* (T)
9 Nov Cenotaph Remembrance Service televised (using tele-recording for first time)
20 Nov Wedding of Princess Elizabeth and Duke of Edinburgh (R & T)

1948

5 Jan *Television Newsreel* (T)
Mrs Dale's Diary (R)
27 Jan *Television Dancing Club* (T) Victor Silvester
23 Mar *Take It From Here* (R)
6 Apr *Inventors Club* (T)
3 Jul *Top of the Form* (R)
29 Jul Olympic Games Wembley (T)
12 Oct *Any Questions?* (R)
26 Dec *Authority and the Individual* (R) First Reith Lecture by Bertrand Russell

1949

31 Jan *Book At Bedtime* (R)
6 May *Billy Cotton's Band Show* (R)
29 Mar Golf televised for first time
4 Apr *Ray's A Laugh* (R) Ted Ray
29 Jul First television weather forecast
24 Oct *Matters of Life and Death* (T)

1950

16 Jan *Listen with Mother* (R)
12 Feb European Broadcasting Union formed
23 Feb General Election results reported on television for first time
23 Apr *Children's Newsreel* (T)
21 May Lime Grove studios opened
26 May *In the News* (T)
11 Jul *Andy Pandy* (T)
27 Aug First live television from the Continent

29 Sept *Come Dancing* (T)
30 Sept First television broadcast from the air
26 Oct First radio and television broadcast from the House of Commons
5 Nov *Life with the Lyons* (R)
8 Nov *International Commentary* (R)

1951

1 Jan *The Archers* (R)
28 May *Crazy People* (R), later *The Goon Show*
16 Jul *What's My Line?* (T)
15 Oct First televised party election programme

1952

15 Feb Funeral of King George VI (R & T)
12 Mar *Science Review* (R)
23 Oct *Animal, Vegetable, Mineral?* (T)
15 Dec *Bill and Ben the Flowerpot Men* (T)

1953

1 Jan National Broadcasting Councils for Scotland & Wales set up. Advisory Councils for Northern Ireland, the Midlands, North and West of England reconstituted
16 Apr First televised Budget broadcast
2 May First Party Political Broadcast on television
2 Jun Coronation of Queen Elizabeth II. Ceremony televised for first time
18 Jul *The Quatermass Experiment* (T)
20 Jul *The Good Old Days* (T)
29 Jul *A Life of Bliss* (R)
1 Nov Anglican Holy Communion televised for first time
11 Nov *Panorama* (T)

1954

11 Jan First weatherman televised
13 Jan *Talking About Music* (R), Antony Hopkins
25 Jan *Under Milk Wood* (R)
19 Mar *Thank You, Ally Pally* (T)
8 Apr *Sportsview* (T)
6 May Roger Bannister's four-minute mile race filmed for *Television Newsreel*
31 May *Hello Playmates* (R) Arthur Askey
6 Jun-4 July First European exchange of television programmes with eight countries involved
5 Jul *News and Newsreel* (T)
7 Oct First televised coverage of a Party Conference

2 Nov *Hancock's Half-Hour* (R)
30 Nov *Churchill at Eighty* (T)
12 Dec *Nineteen Eighty-Four* (T)
21 Dec *Zoo Quest* (T)

1955

7 Jan *The Grove Family* (T)
18 Feb Four MPs protest against 14-Day Rule in *In the News* programme
13 Apr *For Deaf Children* (T) later *Vision On*
2 May First VHF transmitting stations opened
29 Jun *Life with the Lyons* (T)
9 Jul *Dixon of Dock Green* (T)
29 Jul *This Is Your Life* (T)
4 Sept *The Brains Trust* (T)
9 Sept *The Woodentops* (T)
14 Sept *Crackerjack* (T)
22 Sept Start of ITV. *Highlight* (T)
4 Oct *Pick of the Pops* (T)
10 Oct Colour television test transmissions began on 405 lines
31 Dec Television available to 95% of population

1956

26 Jan Winter Olympics first televised
1 Feb First BBC Television commissioned opera
18 Apr *Music for You* (T)
27 Apr First television Ministerial broadcast (Eden as Prime Minister)
22 May *Billy Cotton Band Show* (T)
24 May *Eurovision Song Contest* (T)
6 Jul *Hancock's Half-Hour* (T)
4 Oct *Whack-O!* (T)
3 Nov Eden's ministerial broadcast on Suez
4 Nov Opposition reply by Gaitskell
19 Nov *Lenny the Lion* (T)
18 Dec Postmaster-General announced suspension of 14-Day Rule edict for an experimental six-month period

1957

1 Jan *My Word!* (R)
5 Jan *The Benny Hill Show* (T)
16 Feb *6.5 Special* (T)
18 Feb *Tonight* (T)
22 Feb *On Safari* (T) Armand & Michaela Denis
24 Apr *The Sky at Night* (T)
1 Jun First outside broadcast from Eastern Europe (Prague)
30 Jun *The Restless Sphere* (T) with Prince Philip.

First ball-by-ball Test Match commentary on Third and Light Programmes
25 Jul Prime Minister Macmillan announced 14-Day Rule suspended indefinitely
24 Sept BBC television for schools began
29 Sept *Gardeners' Question Time* (R) on National network. *Does the Team Think?* (R)
30 Sept Reorganisation of Radio Services. Network Three and Regional Television News began
5 Oct *Record Review* (R)
Oct-Nov Transfer of Overseas Service to Bush House
14 Oct Queen Elizabeth's first television broadcast
15 Oct *Lifeline* (T)
20 Oct *Pinky and Perky* (T)
26 Oct *Saturday Night on the Light* (R)
28 Oct *Today* (R)
25 Dec Queen's Christmas Broadcast televised for first time

1958

2 Feb *Monitor* (T)
11 Feb *Your Life in Their Hands* (T)
21 Feb *Press Conference*. First appearance of a Prime Minister (Macmillan) in a regular TV programme
14 Apr Radiophonic Workshop began
5 May Experimental television transmissions on 625 lines began
7 May *White Heather Club* (T)
14 Jun *Black and White Minstrel Show* (T)
1 Jul *Beyond Our Ken* (R) with Kenneth Horne
23 Aug First time starting prices included in horse racing results
1 Oct AMPEX video recording used for first time
11 Oct *Grandstand* (T)
13 Oct *Roundabout* (T)
16 Oct *Blue Peter* (T)
28 Oct State Opening of Parliament first televised by BBC and ITV
4 Nov Coronation of Pope John XXIII televised via Eurovision

1959

4 Jan *Face to Face* (T)
21 Mar *Whicker's World* (T)
1 Apr *The Glory that Was Greece* (T) Compton Mackenzie
3 Apr *Pick of the Week* (R)
1 Jun *Juke Box Jury* (T)
8 Oct General Election campaign covered in news

for first time
12 Nov Cinema premiere of *This is the BBC* (Best Special Film of 1959)
19 Dec BBC electronic field-store converter used for first time

1960

26 Mar Grand National first televised
28 Apr *An Age of Kings* (T)
6 May Princess Margaret's wedding televised and seen by a world audience
20 Jun First female newsreader in vision (Nan Winton)
29 Jun Opening of Television Centre
19 Sept Start of *Ten O'Clock* (R) news and current affairs programme, ending the traditional 9pm news
31 Oct *Maigret* (T)

1961

9 Feb *Gallery* (T)
21 Mar Betting odds information broadcast for first time before a race
14 Apr First television relay from Soviet Union
1 May *Panorama* (T) from Moscow
26 May *Black and White Minstrel Show* (T) won BBC's first Golden Rose of Montreux
29 May First television interview with member of Royal Family. Duke of Edinburgh in *Panorama*
3 Jun *Afternoon Theatre* (R)
10 Jun First live television broadcast to Soviet Union from London (Trooping the Colour)
14 Jun *The Grandeur that Was Rome* (T) Mortimer Wheeler
1 Oct *Songs of Praise* (T)
2 Oct *Points of View* (T)
6 Oct *The Rag Trade* (T)
8 Oct *In Touch* (R)
31 Oct *Television and the World* (T) a documentary by Richard Cawston

1962

2 Jan *Z Cars* (T)
13 Apr *Animal Magic* (T)
7 Jun *Steptoe and Son* (T)
11 Jul First live television from the USA by Telstar satellite
16 Aug *Dr Finlay's Casebook* (T)
28 Aug Experimental stereo radio transmissions began
30 Oct *The Men from the Ministry* (R)
11 Nov *Elgar* (T) Ken Russell

24 **Nov** *That Was The Week That Was* (T)

1963
5 Oct Start of adult educational television on BBC1
23 Nov *Dr Who* (T)
30 Dec *Study Session* on Third Network

1964
1 Jan *Top of the Pops* (T)
19 Apr *Hamlet at Elsinore* (T)
20 Apr BBC2 opened on 625 lines. A power failure spoilt the event
21 Apr *Play School* (T)
24 Apr *Westminster at Work* (T)
26 Apr *News Review for the Deaf* (T) (later *Newsview*)
2 May *Horizon* (T)
30 May *The Great War* (T)
22 Aug *Match of the Day* (T)
28 Oct *The Wednesday Play* (T)
13 Nov *Not So Much a Programme, More a Way of Life* (T)
12 Dec *Jazz Record Requests* (R)
15 Dec *Culloden* (T)

1965
6 Jan *Petticoat Line* (R) with Anona Winn
9 Jan *Not Only....But Also* (T) Peter Cook and Dudley Moore
7 Mar *Round the Horne* (R) with Kenneth Horne
8 Apr *The Wars of the Roses* (T)
1 May General Overseas Service renamed BBC World Service (later to be the name of all the External Services)
2 May *Out of this World* (T) using Early Bird geo-stationary satellite
18 May *Debussy* (T) by Ken Russell
30 May *The World of Wooster* (T)
7 Jul *Tomorrow's World* (T)
Mogul (T) later *The Troubleshooters*
4 Oct *The World at One* (R) *I'm Sorry I'll Read that Again* (R)
10 Oct Start of programme for immigrants (R & T)
17 Oct *Call My Bluff* (T)
18 Oct *Magic Roundabout* (T)
3 Nov *Up the Junction* (T)
13 Dec *Jackanory* (T)

1966
5 Jan *Softly, Softly* (T)

2 Feb *Man Alive* (T)
5 Apr *The Money Programme* (T)
2 Jun First live television pictures from the moon
6 Jun *Till Death Us Do Part* (T)
14 June *Woman's Hour* (R) from Moscow
18 Jun *Chronicle* (T)
30 Jul World Cup Final between England and West Germany televised
7 Aug *It's a Knock Out* (T) (later *Jeux Sans Frontieres*)
16 Nov *Cathy Come Home* (T)
28 Dec *Alice in Wonderland* (T)

1967
3 Jan *My Music!* (R)
7 Jan *The Forsyte Saga* (T)
26 Mar *Frost Over England* (T) with David Frost
6 May *One Pair of Eyes* (T)
25 Jun *Our World* (T), first worldwide live satellite programme
8 Jul *The Old Man of Hoy* (T), an historic outside broadcast
3 Aug *Face the Music* (T)
31 Aug BBC field-store standards converter used for first time for transatlantic colour television
17 Sept *The World this Weekend* (R)
26 Sept *Talkback* (T)
30 Sept Radio 1 started. Former networks renamed Radios 2,3 and 4.
2 Oct *Jimmy Young Show* (R)
13 Oct *Omnibus* (T)
8 Nov Radio Leicester opened, the first local radio station
3 Dec *The World About Us* (T)
22 Dec *Just a Minute* (R)

1968
5 Jan *Gardeners' World* (T)
3 Feb *Aida* (T) from Covent Garden
7 Mar *Newsroom* (T) the first news programme in colour
29 Apr *Marty* (T) with Marty Feldman
31 Jul *Dad's Army* (T)
21 Aug Invasion of Czechoslovakia reported via Eurovision
2 Sept *Morecambe and Wise Show* (T)
12 Sept *Sportsnight with Coleman* (T)
9 Nov *Braden's Week* (T)

1969
2 Jan *Holiday '69* (T)

23 Feb *Civilisation* (T)
1 Mar First broadcast by Prince Charles (on Radio 4)
28 Apr *Waggoners' Walk* (R)
21 Jun *Royal Family* (T)
1 Jul Prince of Wales' Investiture televised
10 July 'Broadcasting in the Seventies' published
18 Jul *The Liver Birds* (T)
21 Jul Armstrong's moon landing televised
22 Jul BBC engineers received Queen's Award to Industry for work on advanced colour standards converter
23 Jul *Pot Black* (T)
9 Sept *Nationwide* (T)
27 Sept *The First Churchills* (T)
5 Oct *Monty Python's Flying Circus* (T)
15 Nov Colour extended to BBC1 and ITV
30 Dec *War and Peace* serialised (R)

1970
1 Jan *The Six Wives of Henry VIII* (T)
9 Feb *Doomwatch* (T)
23 Mar *Up Pompeii!* (T)
4 Apr New pattern of generic radio began. *Week Ending* (R)
6 Apr *Start the Week* (R)
The World Tonight (R)
6 Apr *PM* (R) started
19 Apr *Analysis* (R)
2 Jul State Opening televised in colour for first time
5 Oct *You and Yours* (R)
13 Oct *It's Your Line* (R)

1971
3 Jan Open University programmes began (R & T)
17 Feb *Elizabeth R* (T)
10 Apr *The Two Ronnies* (T)
11 Apr *Blue Peter Royal Safari* (T)
17 Jun *Yesterday's Men* (T)
19 Jun *Parkinson* (T)
21 Sept *The Old Grey Whistle Test* (T)
22 Sept *The Search for the Nile* (T)
2 Oct *Bruce Forsyth and the Generation Game* (T)
3 Oct BBC Programmes Complaints Commission established
15 Oct *The Onedin Line* (T)
15 Nov Princess Anne voted BBC Sports Personality of the Year
21 Nov *The Long March of Everyman* (R)

1972

5 Jan *The Question of Ulster* (T)
11 Jan *The British Empire* (T)
19 Jan Post Office control of broadcasting hours ended
21 Feb *The Regiment* (T)
10 Mar *The Brothers* (T)
4 Apr *Newsround* (T) later *John Craven's Newsround*. The first regular television news programme for children
11 Apr *I'm Sorry I Haven't a Clue* (R)
23 Apr *The Lotus Eaters* (T)
4 Jul *André Previn's Music Night* (T)
11 Sept *Mastermind* (T)
28 Sept *War and Peace* (T)
5 Oct *The Last Goon Show of All* (R)
19 Oct *Colditz* (T)
12 Nov *America* (T) with Alistair Cooke
14 Nov BBC's 50th Anniversary Concert at the Royal Albert Hall
31 Dec *Words* (R)

1973

4 Jan *Last of the Summer Wine* (T)
5 Feb *The Wombles* (T)
14 Mar *Are You Being Served?* (T)
1 Apr *Music Weekly* (R)
2 Apr *Kaleidoscope* (R) *Open Door* (T)
5 May *Ascent of Man* (T)
20 May *M.A.S.H.* (T)
26 May *That's Life!* (T)
6 Jul *Checkpoint* (R)
23 Jul *Radio 1 Road Show* (R)
10 Sept *Newsbeat* (R)
29 Sept *Story of Pop* (R)
8 Oct First ILR station opened
24 Oct *Kojak* (T)
14 Nov Marriage of Princess Anne and Captain Mark Phillips televised to large world audience
24 Nov BBC Radio Carlisle (later renamed Cumbria) opened, completing first 20 local radio stations

1974

3 Jan *It Ain't Half Hot Mum* (T)
19 Jan *The Pallisers* (T)
29 Mar Home Office takes over responsibility for broadcasting from Ministry of Posts and Telecommunications
Apr BBC engineers won Queen's Award to Industry for sound-in-sync system, an early

application of digitalisation
10 Apr Home Secretary announces setting up of Annan Committee
11 May *Science Now* (R)
30 Apr *The Family* (T)
5 Sept *Porridge* (T)
23 Sept Regular CEEFAX service started
28 Sept *Stop the Week* (R)
31 Oct *Leeds United* (T)
30 Dec *Churchill's People* (T)

1975

4 Apr *The Good Life* (T)
31 May *Jim'll Fix It* (T)
9 Jun Start of four-day experiment of radio broadcasts from House of Commons
11 Sept *Days of Hope* (T)
14 Sept *The Explorers* (T)
19 Sept *Fawlty Towers* (T)
1 Oct *Arena* (T)
5 Oct *Poldark* (T)
12 Oct *On the Move* (T) BBC Education adult literacy project started

1976

4 Jan *Quote....Unquote* (R)
8 Jan *When the Boat Comes In* (T)
21 Jan *The Glittering Prizes* (T)
17 Feb *One Man and His Dog* (T)
20 Feb *Open All Hours* (T)
23 Apr *Starsky and Hutch* (T)
5 Aug *Sailor* (T)
3 Sept *A Good Read* (R)
4 Sept *The Duchess of Duke Street* (T)
8 Sept *The Fall and Rise of Reginald Perrin* (T)
20 Sept *I, Claudius* (T)
10 Oct *You the Jury* (R)
3 Nov *The News Huddlines* (R) Roy Hudd

1977

13 Feb *Vivat Rex* (R)
10 Apr *Everyman* (T)
21 Apr *Royal Heritage* (T)
6 Jul *Brass Tacks* (T)
8 Jul *Going Places* (R)
29 Jul Licence fee fixed for one year only
6 Sept *The News Quiz* (R)
19 Sept *The Long Search* (T)
1 Oct *Does He Take Sugar?* (R)
2 Oct *Money Box* (R) *International Assignment* (R)
26 Oct *File on 4* (R)

1978

8 Jan *All Creatures Great and Small* (T)
19 Jan *Men of Ideas* (T)
7 Feb *Young Musician of the Year* (T)
8 Feb *Grange Hill* (T)
7 Mar *Pennies from Heaven* (T)
8 Mar *Hitchhiker's Guide to the Galaxy* (R)
3 Apr Start of regular service of radio broadcasting from House of Commons
6 Apr *Law and Order* (T)
31 Oct *The Voyage of Charles Darwin* (T)
10 Nov *Butterflies* (T)
23 Nov Major LW/MW frequency changes made following 1974/5 Geneva Conference. Allowed increase in number and power of transmitters in Europe. Radio Scotland, Scottish national radio network began broadcasting. Radio 2 became first UK network to broadcast regularly throughout the night.
3 Dec *Romeo and Juliet* (T) Start of BBC Shakespeare project

1979

7 Jan *Telford's Change* (T)
8 Jan *The White Tribe of Africa* (T)
16 Jan *Life on Earth* (T)
18 Feb *Antiques Roadshow* (T)
21 Mar Publication of BBC working party report on Violence on Television; new guidelines laid down for programme-makers
1 Apr *Feedback* (R)
22 Apr *Heart of the Matter* (T)
25 Aug *Big Band Special* (R)
2 Sept First programme with CEEFAX subtitling broadcast
6 Sept *Fred Dibnah, Steeplejack* (T)
10 Sept *Tinker, Tailor, Soldier, Spy* (T)
23 Sept *Churchill and the Generals* (T)
25 Sept *Question Time* (T)
29 Sept *Breakaway* (R)
30 Sept *The Food Programme* (R) *To the Manor Born* (T) *Shoestring* (T)
16 Oct *Not the Nine O'Clock News* (T)
4 Nov *Testament of Youth* (T)
5 Nov *The Magic of Dance* (T)
25 Nov *Suez 1956* (T)

1980

2 Jan *Mainly for Pleasure* (R)
30 Jan *Newsnight* (T)

25 Feb *Yes Minister* (T)
Feb Publication of 'The Portrayal of Violence on Television' (BBC/IBA Guidelines)
1 Apr *Medicine Now* (R)
30 Aug *Juliet Bravo* (T)
11 Sept Radio Norfolk opened, first of a new wave of BBC local radio stations
21 Sept *Shock of the New* (T)
1 Nov *Did You See?* (T)
21 Nov First major TV *Children In Need* appeal
2 Dec *Ireland: A Television History* (T)

1981
26 Feb *Hi-de-Hi!* (T)
8 Mar *The Lord of the Rings* (R)
1 Jun Broadcasting Complaints Commission established under Broadcasting Act 1980
1 Jul *Three of a Kind* (T)
21 Jul Broadcasters' Audience Research Board (BARB) set up
29 Jul Wedding of Prince of Wales and Lady Diana Spencer; seen in 74 countries (R & T)
8 Sept *Only Fools and Horses* (T)
20 Sept *Priestland's Progress* (R)
1 Oct *40 Minutes* (T)
14 Oct *The Borgias* (T)
18 Oct *Bergerac* (T)
22 Oct *Tenko* (T)
23 Oct First meeting of National Broadcasting Council for Northern Ireland

1982
Jan Start of BBC Education Computer Literacy Project, BBC Microcomputer introduced
14 Feb *Flight of the Condor* (T)
4 Mar Government announced BBC would be authorised to start broadcasting two satellite services in 1986
7 Apr *Rough Justice* (T)
14 May Official opening of BBC/OU Production Centre at Milton Keynes by Prince of Wales
31 Jul *In the Psychiatrist's Chair* (R)
29 Sept *Timewatch* (T)
2 Oct *Carrott's Lib* (T)
10 Oct *The Boys from the Blackstuff* (T)
17 Oct *The Ring* (T)
1 Nov BBC Welsh-language programmes transferred to Sianel 4

1983
17 Jan BBC breakfast television transmissions began

7 Feb *When the Wind Blows* (R)
3 Mar *The Paras* (T)
21 Apr BBC Engineering Division and IBA Engineering won Queen's Award for teletext developments
15 Jun *Blackadder* (T)
28 Sept *Bookmark* (T)
29 Nov *An Englishman Abroad* (T)

1984
8 Jan *The Thorn Birds* (T)
19 Jan *The Living Planet* (T)
30 Jan *Panorama (Maggie's Militant Tendency)* (T)
31 Jan *Alas, Smith and Jones* (T)
13 Apr *All Our Working Lives* (T)
6 May *It's Your World* (R) live phone-in to world leaders on World Service and Radio 4
7 Jun *Crimewatch* (T)
24 Jul *On the Air* (R)
4 Sept *Lenny Henry Show* (T)
7 Sept *'Allo, 'Allo* (T)
26 Dec *Miss Marple* (T)

1985
11 Jan *Victoria Wood as Seen on TV* (T)
23 Jan Start of six-month experiment of televising proceedings of House of Lords
18 Feb *Wogan* (T)
19 Feb *EastEnders* (T)
17 Apr *After Henry* (R)
8 Jul Direct Broadcast by Satellite consortium wound up
13 Jul *Live Aid* (T)
14 Jul *Watchdog* (T)
21 Jul *Drugwatch* (T)
17 Aug *The Observer* carried story about alleged BBC vetting by MI5
1 Sept *Howards' Way* (T)
9 Sept *Triumph of the West* (T)
16 Oct *Real Lives: At the Edge of the Union* (T)
17 Nov *Comrades* (T)

1986
4 Jan *Loose Ends* (R)
10 Jan *Lovejoy* (T)
17 Feb *Hospital Watch* (T)
27 Feb *The Fishing Party* (T) in *40 Minutes* series
1 Apr All BBC commercial activities brought together in a single organisation, BBC Enterprises Ltd
1 May *Bread* (T)

31 Aug *The Monocled Mutineer* (T)
6 Sept *Casualty* (T)
13 Oct *The Clothes Show* (T)
27 Oct Daytime Television service launched. *Neighbours* (T)
30 Oct *Childwatch* (T)
1 Nov BBC English Regional reorganisation announced
13 Nov Publication of BBC 'Violence on Television' report
16 Nov *The Singing Detective* (T)
1 Dec *Antenna* (T)

1987
31 Jan Police raid BBC Glasgow and remove *Secret Society* programmes and files
9 Mar *French and Saunders* (T)
21 Apr BBC Engineering and Electricity Council received Queen's Award for Radio Teleswitching
6 Aug BBC and IBA agree to Government proposal for 25% independent programming
11 Oct *Fortunes of War* (T)
12 Oct *Kilroy* (T)
27 Oct *Citizens* (R)
5 Nov *Punters* (R)

1988
3 Jan *See For Yourself* (T)
18 Jan *Third Ear* (R)
1 Apr Licence fee pegged to Retail Price Index
19 Apr *Talking Heads* (T)
9 May *Def II* (T) strand for youth
16 May Home Secretary announces setting up of Broadcasting Standards Council
31 May *Tumbledown* (T)
4 Jul *Rough Guide to Europe* (T)
1 Sept BBC External Services renamed World Service
18 Sept *On the Record* (T)
20 Sept Radio Data System (RDS) officially launched
19 Oct Government bans sound-plus-vision broadcasts of statements supporting organisations associated with terrorism in Northern Ireland
30 Oct *All in the Mind* (R)
13 Nov *Chronicles of Narnia* (T)

1989
7 Jan *Age to Age* (R)
16 Jan *The Late Show* (T)

21 Jan *Saturday Night Clive* (T)
1 Mar BBC issued comprehensive new guidelines for producers
16 Oct *Birds of a Feather* (T)
20 Oct *Public Eye* (T)
7 Nov Granada sells *What the Papers Say* (T) to the BBC
11 Nov *Europhile* (R)
21 Nov Start of experimental televising of House of Commons

1990

1 Jan BBC Subscription Television Service created as a separate company within BBC Enterprises Ltd
4 Jan *One Foot in the Grave* (T)
10 Jan *Oranges Are Not the Only Fruit* (T)
25 Jan BBC 'Funding the Future' report presented
5 Feb Time pips from Greenwich heard for last time
27 Mar *Troubleshooter* (T)
5 May *Berlin Weekend* (R)
19 Jul MPs voted to approve televising of proceedings of House of Commons
27 Aug Radio 5 began
5 Sept White City building handed over to BBC
19 Sept *Portrait of a Marriage* (T)
28 Sept *Have I Got News for You* (T)
29 Sept *Forsyte Chronicles* (R)
3 Oct *Trials of Life* (T)
1 Nov Broadcasting Act received Royal Assent
12 Nov Richard Dimbleby became first broadcaster to be honoured with a memorial plaque in Westminster Abbey

1991

3 Jan Last issue of *The Listener* published
8 Jan *Spender* (T)
11 Mar World Service Television News service started
1 Apr Licence fee pegged below rate of inflation
15 Apr World Service Television started
31 May *Second Russian Revolution* (T)
1 Jun *Twin Cities Weekend* (R)
31 Jul Lime Grove studios closed
31 Aug Start of BBC TV NICAM stereo sound services
16 Sept *The Bible* (R)
5 Oct *Japan Season* (R)
14 Oct World Service Television launched Asian Service, which later became first BBC 24-hour TV channel
27 Nov *Clarissa* (T)

1992

21 Jan Launch of night-time BBC TV Select Service. Radio Berkshire opened, the last of the BBC chain of local radio stations
26 Jan 50th anniversary of *Desert Island Discs* (R) with the Prime Minister, John Major
6 Feb *Elizabeth R* (T) documentary on The Queen
1 Mar *Truly, Madly, Deeply*
26 Apr *Hamlet* (R)
4 May First foreign language World Service Television broadcast in Mandarin
1 Jun Start of Ukrainian Service
28 June National Music Day (R)
6 July *Eldorado*
14 July Sir Michael Checkland announces plans for a 24-hour radio news network, a News and Current Affairs complex at Television Centre and a new Education Directorate

Further Reading

The number of books now available on BBC broadcasting history is considerable, ranging from the scholastic to the light-hearted. The selection below is intended for those who wish to begin filling in the outline provided in this book. The first four titles on broadcasting history have extensive bibliographies.

1 *The History of Broadcasting in the United Kingdom* by Briggs A. is the standard and most comprehensive account up to the mid-Fifties. It comes in four volumes, all at present out of print, but available in good libraries, published by the Oxford University Press.

Vol I	The Birth of Broadcasting (1961)
Vol II	The Golden Age of Wireless (1965)
Vol III	The War of Words (1970)
Vol IV	Sound and Vision (1979)
Vol V	which takes the story up to the mid-Seventies is in course of completion.

2 *The BBC: The First Fifty Years* by Briggs A. (OUP 1985) is a single-volume account covering the years 1922 to 1972. It is available in good libraries, and an updated version is in preparation.

3 *A Social History of British Broadcasting Volume One 1922-39* by Scannell P. and Cardiff D. (Blackwell 1991) is an excellent account of aspects of early BBC history.

4 *Let Truth Be Told* by Mansell G. (Weidenfeld and Nicolson 1982) is an authoritative account of the history of the BBC World Service from the beginning of the Empire Service up to the Seventies.

5 *A Skyful of Freedom* by Walker A. (Broadside Books 1992) is a shorter, more personal account of 60 years of the BBC World Service.

6 The BBC Handbooks and Yearbooks, published for many years, are invaluable sources of information. Now called *BBC Annual Report and Accounts*, the 1991/92 edition is available with a BBC Guide and contains an up-to-date bibliography.

7 *Governing the BBC* by Briggs A. (BBC 1979) is primarily about the constitutional role of BBC Governors, but contains detailed case study accounts of controversies which involved the Governors.

8 Some Directors-General and Chairmen have written revealingly about BBC broadcasting. Among these are:-
A Seamless Robe Curran C. (Collins 1978)
The Third Floor Front Greene H. (Bodley Head 1969)
Behind the Screen Lord Hill of Luton (Sidgwick and Jackson 1974)

Into the Wind Reith J.C.W. (Hodder and Stoughton 1949)
Broadcast Over Britain Reith J.C.W. (Hodder and Stoughton 1924) is a statement of Reith's broadcasting philosophy.
The BBC From Within Lord Simon of Wythenshawe (Gollancz 1953)
Split Screen Trethowan I. (Hamish Hamilton 1984)
D G: The Memoirs of a British Broadcaster Milne A. (Hodder 1988)

9 *British Broadcasting* Smith A. (ed.) (David & Charles 1974) This is a collection of extracts from over 100 key broadcasting documents.

10 *The Most Contrary Region, the BBC in Northern Ireland 1924-84* Cathcart R. (Blackstaff Press 1984)

11 *BBC Engineering 1922-72* - Pawley E. (BBC 1972) By a former Chief Engineer, External Relations.

12 *Who's Listening? The Story of BBC Audience Research* Silvey R. (Allen and Unwin 1977) By the first Head of BBC Audience Research.

13 *Learning Over the Air: 60 Years of Partnership in Adult Education* Robinson J. (BBC 1982)

14 *The BBC: Public institution and Private World* Burns T. (Macmillan 1977) The view of a sociologist.

15 *The Biggest Aspidistra in the World: A personal celebration of fifty years of the BBC* Black P. BBC 1972 The view of a distinguished critic.

16 *The Radio Companion* Donovan P. (Harper Collins 1991)

17 *Early Wireless* Constable A. (Midas 1980)

18 *Television: A History* Wheen F. (Century 1985)

19 *Here's Looking at You The Story of British Television 1908-37* - Norman B. (BBC/RTS 1984)

20 *The BBC Symphony Orchestra 1930-80* Kenyon N. (BBC 1981)

21 *Laughter in the Air: An Informal History of British Radio Comedy* - Took B. (Robson 1981)

22 *The Churches and the British Broadcasting Corporation 1922-56* Wolfe K.M. (SCM 1984)

23 *Facing the Nation: Television and Politics 1936-76* Grace Wyndham Goldie (The Bodley Head 1977) By an ex-Head of BBC Television Talks and Current Affairs)

24 *Broadcasting in the UK: A Guide to Information Sources* MacDonald B. (Mansell 1988)

Index

References to programmes and illustrations are indicated by italic page numbers.